THE
ELEMENTS
OF
COUNSELING

THE
ELEMENTS
OF
COUNSELING

Scott T. Meier

State University of New York at Buffalo

89-495

Brooks/Cole Publishing Company
Pacific Grove, California

Brooks/Cole Publishing Company
A Division of Wadsworth, Inc.

© 1989 by Wadsworth, Inc., Belmont, California 94002.

Printed in the United States of America

10 9 8 7 6 5 4 3 2 1

Library of Congress Cataloging in Publication Data

Meier, Scott T., [date]
The elements of counseling/Scott T. Meier.
p. cm.
Bibliography: p.
Includes index.
ISBN 0-534-09900-9
1. Counseling.   I. Title.
BF637.C6M42   1988   158 .3—dc19   68-18754CIP

Sponsoring Editor: *Claire Verduin*
Marketing Representative: *Dawn Beke*
Editorial Assistant: *Gay C. Bond*
Production Editor: *Linda Loba*
Production Assistant: *Marie DuBois*
Permissions Editor: *Carline Haga*
Interior and Cover Design: *Kelly Shoemaker*
Printing and Binding: *Malloy Lithographing, Inc.*

Preface

Strunk and White's (1979) *The Elements of Style,* a basic introduction to English composition, provided the model for this book. As White notes in his introduction, Strunk originally composed *The Elements of Style* to "cut the vast tangle of English rhetoric down to size and write its rules and principles on the head of a pin." Strunk, a university English instructor, attempted to produce a set of rules to help students avoid basic mistakes in composition. My purpose is similar: distill the basic elements of counseling and teach what counseling is as well as what it is *not.*

Describing counseling's basic elements is a difficult task. In these preparadigmatic days (Staats, 1983; Kuhn, 1962), counseling lacks a strong consensus about such fundamental issues as the integration of diverse counseling approaches (Ivey, 1980), the usefulness of counseling research to practice (Goldman, 1976; Gelso, 1979), and the specific interaction between various client characteristics and counseling approaches (Krumboltz, 1966). More than 400 types of psychotherapy are said to be operating (Karasu, 1986). This lack of consensus makes sense, given the youth of the helping professions and the complexity of the undertaking. Moreover, this disunity is shared by most other branches of psychology and the social sciences (see Meier, 1987). It is important to note that the profession *does* possess a knowledge base; however, theory, research, and practice in counseling often appear fragmented and contradictory.

The issue of disunity is long-standing (see Rogers, 1963; Gelso, 1979; Forsyth & Strong, 1986), but I bring up the debate because I believe disunity remains a major impediment to progress in the profession. *What* metatheories of counseling eventually develop are probably not so important as *how* they are constructed and presented. Elsewhere (Meier, 1987) I have proposed that an integrated theory should possess four major attributes: (a) the theory should be interconnected, thereby bridging diverse approaches; (b) the theory should be surprising and make strong, unexpected predictions that intrigue counseling researchers; (c) the theory should be readily applicable, specific enough to permit derivation of a technology of counseling; and (d) the theory should be aesthetically pleasing so as to appeal to current artisans and practitioners of counseling.

If there is so much disunity in counseling, what is there to teach in a basic elements book? My sense is that much of the disagreement centers on counseling interventions; counselors share greater agreement about the initial stages of counseling. For example, most counselors would agree that information must be gathered about the client and some degree of rapport established between client and counselor. Building on the work of others, this book represents my attempt at delineating these basic elements of counseling practice. Consequently, *The Elements of Counseling* focuses on relationship building and self-exploration, the foundation upon which further intervention is laid.

Whereas some agreement exists among counselors about initial counseling practices, little consensus has been reached about the timing, sequence, or relative importance of these practices (see Goldfried, 1983; Cormier & Cormier, 1985). Thus, different counselors and counseling instructors might rearrange substantial portions of this book to suit their preferences and experiences. That makes sense: this book could be read in sections or in sequence like a textbook. But this book, like the counseling profession, needs an underlying foundation.

The Elements of Counseling may be useful for graduate students in the helping professions (such as psychiatry, psychology, social work, and counseling), as well as for paraprofessionals and peer counselors who are learning basic counseling, communications, and listening skills. Undergraduate students enrolled in introductory psychology or counseling courses may find that the book contributes to an understanding of the applied aspects of psychology. I also hope experienced counselors and psychotherapists find these ideas to be valuable reminders.

Although *The Elements of Counseling* presents guidelines and rules, one cannot become a counselor simply by memorizing them. Given the necessarily brief nature of *The Elements of Counseling*, students may overestimate or underestimate their capabilities if they only read this book. Practice in role plays, actual experience, competent supervision, and development of a personal counseling theory are the requisites for competent counselors. Likewise, no claim can be made that this book exhaustively lists all the basics of counseling. *The Elements of Counseling* is designed to function as a brief reference tool. I hope that what the book lacks in comprehensiveness it atones for in simplicity, clarity, and brevity.

The Elements of Counseling has about 30 coauthors. Those persons include past teachers, supervisors, colleagues, and students—the persons who taught me about the elements of counseling. Thank you all. I also acknowledge the helpful comments and suggestions of more immediate colleagues and teachers: Drs. Diane Gale, Susan Chiddix, James Hansen, Robert Rossberg, the book's reviewers (Prof. Virginia Allen, Idaho State University; Dr. Susan Anzivino, University of Maine; Dr. Sheryl Bartholomew, SUNY-Oswego; Dr. Bianca Bernstein, Arizona State University; Dr. David E. Botwin, University of Pittsburgh; Dr. Mari Irvin, University of the Pacific; Dr. William A. Lewis, University of Missouri; Dr. Anthony LoGuidice, Frostburg State University, Maryland), David Steinweg and other SUNYAB counseling psychology students, and the editor, Claire Verduin. Finally, I thank my partner, Dr. Susan Davis, for her ideas, feedback, and suggestions.

Scott T. Meier

Contents

CHAPTER 1

. . . .

An Approach to Counseling Process

Process produces outcome. The process of counseling—what the counselor and client do in session—influences the outcome, the success of counseling. To master process, beginning counselors must develop a repertoire of helping skills, as well as a theory of counseling that directs their application.

How do you go about developing an approach to process? This is no easy task: a recent estimate placed the number of different counseling approaches (such as psychoanalytic, behavioral, and rational-emotive) at more than 400 (Karasu, 1986). Research on psychotherapy outcome shows no broad superiority for any one approach (Smith & Glass, 1977), and no theoretical consensus has yet been negotiated among the major schools.

Needless to say, many contemporary counselors describe themselves as eclectic. At its best, eclectic counseling involves *doing what works*. Given their training in a wide variety of counseling approaches, eclectic counselors rationally and intuitively select an approach based on the individual needs of their clients. In some cases, this matching process is straightforward. For example, if a client appears at your office with a simple phobia, you could employ systematic desensitization with a strong expectation for success (Wolpe, 1982). However, the match between client and approach is often unclear, and in these instances the weakness of eclecticism is exposed. At its worst, then, eclectic counseling involves guessing or flying by the seat of your pants.

I offer here 12 methods, derived from research and counseling practice, that counselors use to begin and strengthen a helping relationship. Students who master these steps will have acquired a repertoire of basic helping skills.

1. Make personal contact.

The foundation of counseling is the relationship between counselor and client. Different approaches emphasize the counseling relationship to varying degrees, but all practitioners understand that the client and the counselor must first make contact.

Because counselors lack a precise method for describing relationships between people, *making personal contact* is difficult to describe. We have to talk around the topic: making contact means being with the client, touching someone emotionally, communicating. This does not mean clients must immediately develop an intense relationship with the counselor. In fact, the contact may need to be moderate for clients afraid of intimacy and personal contact.

Pay particular attention to making contact with your clients during the first session (see Gunzburger, Henggeler, & Watson, 1985; Sullivan, 1970; Pope, 1979). Be open to your clients' lead. If they start to chat, chat for a minute, then return to the business of counseling.

Counselor:	Hi, I'm Susan. I'm your counselor.
Client:	Hello, I'm Bill. It certainly is snowing hard out there.
Counselor:	(*contact!*) Yes, it is. Did you have any trouble getting here?
Counselor:	(*too direct*) Let's talk about your problems, not the snow.

Allowing your clients to lead in the initial stages of counseling encourages the development of trust. It also provides information about clients' agendas and their interpersonal styles (MacKinnon & Michels, 1971, cited in Pope, 1979).

What could stop you from making personal contact? For example, I start to feel rushed if I see too many clients consecutively. To avoid this effect, I set aside 10 to 15 minutes between clients to take notes from the previous session and review notes in preparation for the next hour. Resting between sessions enables me to attend to each client as a unique individual.

2. Develop a working alliance.

Making personal contact is the first step in developing a working alliance (Greenson, 1965; Zetzel, 1956). The task of the counselor is to engage the client in such a way that both persons are working together to resolve the issues that brought the client to counseling (Davis, 1987). Such alliances do *not* occur, for example, when the counselor attempts to force the client to change or when the client is unmotivated.

Counselors invite their clients into this working alliance by extending understanding, respect, and warmth. Thus, counselors must be skilled interpersonally.

Client:	I'm at the end of my rope. I'm so frustrated!
Counselor:	This is *really* a difficult time for you.
Client:	It feels good to hear you say that. None of my friends understand what I'm going through.

Counselors are skilled listeners. By learning about clients through attentive listening, and offering acceptance of clients as they are, counselors develop a bond of trust and support. Without this alliance, many clients are unable to change.

3. Explain counseling to the client.

Researchers call the explanatory step *role induction* (Orlinsky & Howard, 1978; Hoehn-Saric, Frank, Imber, Nash, Stone, & Battle, 1964; Mayerson, 1984). Clients frequently approach counseling with misconceptions about the process. For example, they may expect counseling to resemble a visit to a medical doctor: diagnosis, prescription, cure. If mistaken expectations are ignored, clients may drop out or fail to make progress.

Client:	Doc, why aren't you asking me more questions about my mental illness?
Counselor:	John, I see counseling being most helpful when you're talking with me about your feelings. That's the best way for both of us to learn about what's going on with you.
Client:	Well . . . okay.

In this example the client expected the counselor to lead the counseling session by asking questions. The counselor explained, in essence, that it was the client's job to talk and that exploring feelings was the current task of counseling.

Beginning counselors should avoid explanations until they feel comfortable and knowledgeable enough to make them. Practice first in role plays. *What* to explain depends on such factors as presenting problem or agency policies; for example, it may be unnecessary to describe the limits of confidentiality regarding potential homicide to a student seeking career counseling. Clients may find it helpful, however, to know that (a) they will do most of the talking, (b) they may experience painful feelings before they begin to feel better, (c) exceptions exist regarding the confidentiality of counseling, (d) persons in counseling are not inherently weak, and (e) most individuals in counseling are quite sane.

Clients may also find it helpful to know that they may take some time to find a resolution to their problems. Many clients approach their first session hoping to find an immediate solution.

Client:	I'm glad we could meet today. I'm going home this weekend and my father wants to know what my major is and what kind of job I'm going to get when I graduate.
Counselor:	Sounds like you're under pressure to make a quick choice.
Client:	Sort of—he keeps asking me about it and I just want to be able to tell him something.

Counselor:	We might be better off to spend more than 50 minutes deciding on your major and your career. It's important to explore your abilities and interests as well as job requirements.
Client:	I guess so.
Counselor:	It might also make sense to talk about how your father will react to your decisions.
Client:	That's true.

In this example the counselor provided the client with permission to take more time, as well as a rationale for why the extra time might be useful.

Role induction may be part of a set of procedures designed to increase clients' expectations for therapeutic gain (Frank, 1971). Clients' (and therapists') belief in the effectiveness of counseling affects outcome (Rosenthal & Frank, 1958; also see Orlinsky & Howard, 1978, pp. 300-304). Part of your job, then, is to provide clients with realistic hope for improvement.

Client:	I'm getting so afraid of snakes that I won't leave the house much any more.
Counselor:	The approach we're going to use—called systematic desensitization—has proven highly effective for eliminating phobias like your fear of snakes.
Client:	Okay . . . what do we do?

In this example the counselor described the counseling procedure and its past effectiveness. However, once you become skilled at explaining counseling to your clients, you may be tempted to explain *everything*. This places the counselor in the foreground and encourages clients to hide behind intellectualizations.

Client:	After we argued, I went home and kicked the dog. Is that reaction formation or displacement?

| Counselor: | Displacement. Instead of expressing your anger to your boss you expressed it to your dog. |
| Client: | Right. I thought it was displacement, but I wasn't sure. |

Here the counselor has taken on the position of expert and allowed the client to remove the focus from herself. As an alternative, the counselor might inquire how that knowledge (of classifying "kicking the dog" as reaction formation or displacement) would help the client.

Role induction is one way of organizing or structuring counseling (Shertzer & Stone, 1980). Counselors vary in the amount of structure they place on the counseling process, but most professionals at least perform an initial interview (to gather information about the presenting problem and background), set goals (to determine when counseling will be complete), build the counseling relationship and explore client issues, implement an intervention, and finally, terminate the relationship.

4. Pace and lead the client.

Pacing and leading refer to how much direction the counselor exerts with the client. When pacing a client, a counselor follows along in terms of the client's expressed content and feeling.

Client:	(*sighing*) I put off studying until the last minute again, and then I just hit the books the whole night.
Counselor:	You crammed again.
Client:	Yeah. That's what happened.

Here the counselor paced the client by succinctly restating the client's concern. Nothing was added to the client's meaning; no direction was given. Pacing lets the client know that the counselor is listening and understanding.

Reflection of feeling and *restatement of content* (Egan, 1986) are two effective methods of pacing clients. Reflection of feeling refers to the counselor's recognition of the client's feeling and a subsequent mirroring of that feeling. With restatement of content, the counselor notices the client's thoughts and restates the content. Reflection of feeling and restatement of content build rapport between counselor and client by developing a consensus about what the client is thinking and feeling. For many people, having another person listen deeply makes those experiences more real. In fact, some clients seem unaware of what they are experiencing until they hear a restatement or paraphrase.

Client:	I was so mad I just got up and left.
Counselor:	You were really angry with your husband.
Client:	Yes . . . I guess I was. I just realized how angry I was—and still am!

Pacing and leading are another way of discussing *timing*. Through experience and through watching the individual reactions of clients, counselors develop a sense of when they should direct the counseling process.

Client:	I'm stuck. I just can't keep putting off studying like this.
Counselor:	I wonder if your cramming has anything to do with your desire to avoid responsibility for failing the course.
Client:	Well . . . my dad thinks I get C's because I party like he did in college, not because I don't have the ability. Hmmm. . . .
Counselor:	(*silence*)

In this example the counselor intervened at a point when she believed the client was ready to hear a new message. Once the client made the connection, the counselor backed off and allowed the client to think about the new material.

Psychologically sophisticated clients progress more quickly because of their greater familiarity with the counseling process. Highly motivated clients can better tolerate the pain and ambiguity often present during the course of counseling.

Strong rapport also signals the counselor to move ahead on client issues.

Counselor:	We've spent several sessions speaking about how you can adjust to your illness ... but we haven't spoken about death.
Client:	I know.
Counselor:	(*silence*)
Client:	I know ... I know I have to start talking about dying.

The counselor recognized this individual's self-awareness of his fear of death and gently brought it to his attention. The client's awareness of the importance of talking about that fear helped him to begin the process.

Pacing occurs most naturally when client and counselor share such characteristics as socioeconomic status, personal values, cultural background, and life experiences. Similarity encourages understanding based on intuitive insight into the other's experience. The effectiveness of peer counseling (Varenhorst, 1984), group counseling (Yalom, 1985), and paraprofessional counselors (Durlak, 1979) may be due partially to the pacing that occurs naturally in such homogeneous settings. The status of professionally trained counselors may increase credibility, but at a cost to their capacity to match and pace clients.

An important contraindication for leading is *your* state of stress. Stressed counselors may be too inclined to take risks and push their clients (Freudenberger, 1974; Meier, 1983; for an introduction to the area of impaired professionals, see Kilburg, Nathan, & Thoresen, 1986). In general, when counselors lead too much they lose their clients, figuratively and literally. Introducing three or four major insights during one session may seem like brilliant counselor strategy, but clients are likely to remember only one or two themes. Leading clients into a sensitive area too soon can be risky. One beginning counselor felt he had zeroed in on his client's major issues and began to share his interpretations during the first session. He assumed the client would recognize the truth of these insights and change. Instead, the client became frightened and dropped out of counseling.

5. *Speak briefly.*

In general, counselors should talk less than their clients. Except when summarizing, communicate in one or two sentences. Unfortunately, even the best counselors can get carried away.

Client: My dad got angry at me, so I went to the store and got something to eat.

Counselor: So your father lost his temper again, and as usual, you got a stomach ache when you started to feel anxious about your dad's yelling. I wonder if you were eating as a way to manage your anxiety or whether you just needed to get out of the house. Is there something else you can do to change that the next time your dad becomes angry?

In this example the counselor shared all of her interpretations and solutions at once. If you were the client, how would you feel under this bombardment of questions?

Beginning counselors typically have difficulty being brief with talkative clients. After a goal or theme has been established (for example, to discuss the client's relationship with his father), it's okay to bring a wandering client back to the main issue.

Client: So when my dad yelled at me for the third time that day, I really started to feel anxious. I went down to the corner market and bought something to eat so my stomach wouldn't hurt so much. I didn't want to study, so I called my boyfriend from the store phone and we got into an argument. I haven't talked to him since then but I'm wondering if—

Counselor: Could we stop a moment and talk about your feelings about your father?

One technique counselors employ to show they are listening and yet stay out of the client's way is *minimal encouragers* (see

Egan, 1986). Minimal encouragers are phrases like "uh-huh" and nonverbal gestures like head nods.

Client:	I know I have to start talking about my illness.
Counselor:	Yes.
Client:	And it's hard to think straight with the pain. It hurts my family to see me in pain.
Counselor:	(*nodding*)
Client:	They want so badly to help me that we haven't even begun to say good-bye.

This counselor's use of minimal encouragers appears effortless. Nevertheless, the client may be benefiting a great deal from exploring personal issues without counselor interruption.

6. When you don't know what to say, say nothing.

Particularly in counseling, silence is golden. Perhaps because silence can indicate awkwardness in social conversations, beginning counselors often feel uncomfortable with silence and quickly fill the gaps between client statements.

Client:	So I got laid off after 15 years of service.
Counselor:	Fifteen years of hard work . . .
Client:	Yeah . . . (*silence*)
Counselor:	And you're pretty angry at the company too, I imagine.

The client might have been feeling angry, but could also have been experiencing sadness about the job loss or happiness about job accomplishments. However, the counselor's premature statement effectively stopped the client's internal processing of thoughts and feelings. Learn to notice when people are absorbed and dealing with their issues—a sign of real work in counseling.

Apart from the initial interview, it is largely the client's job to talk, not the counselor's. The counselor may sit quietly during silent periods and wait for the client to resume speaking. The best therapists, like good referees in sporting events, work in the background. Referees and therapists tend to be most noticed when they are making mistakes.

Client:	After I failed that exam I was so angry that—
Counselor:	You wanted to drop out of school again.
Client:	—uh . . . no, I wanted to try twice as hard next time.

Not only did the counselor in this example interrupt, but he was wrong; the former is more serious. Counselors think of themselves as helpers. Listening helps, too—sometimes all the help clients need.

7. You may confront as much as you've supported.

Confrontation in counseling does not mean opposing the client, but pointing out discrepancies between clients' goals and their actions (Shertzer & Stone, 1980). In a way, confronting the client is a way of saying, "Stop a minute! Look at what you're doing."

Beginning counselors typically find confrontation difficult. A good rule of thumb is that you can confront as much as you've supported.

Client:	I just don't have the willpower to eat more.
Counselor:	I'm puzzled by that, Joe. When you started counseling two months ago you said that you *really* wanted to get back to your normal weight. That sounded like "willpower" to me.
Client:	Well . . . I do want to gain weight. I just can't do it.

Counselor: What's stopping you?

Support and empathy are the foundation upon which the counseling relationship is built. Consequently, confrontation is unwise during the early stages of counseling. However, once you establish a bond, confrontation may increase client self-awareness and motivation to change (Egan, 1986).

8. If you want to change something, process it.

At this chapter's beginning I described process as what occurs during the counseling session. Counselors also employ the word "process" to describe the act of *talking about* something that is happening in session. Thus, processing refers to discussion of client and counselor feelings about an event or aspect of the counseling relationship.

Counselors contrast *process* with *content* (Pope, 1979), the latter referring to the overt topic of the conversation.

Client: The problems in my marriage are all my wife's fault.

Counselor: She has . . .

Client: (*content*) Started a job. She's not spending any time with me or the kids anymore.

The content in the above example has to do with the client's belief that his wife is the cause of his problems. In contrast, a process comment often focuses on immediacy—that is, what the client and counselor are *feeling and experiencing at that moment.*

Client: I don't know what else to say.

Counselor: (*process*) Seems like it's difficult for you to talk with me.

Client: Yeah. My wife told me I should see you.

Counselor: (*process*) So you're not here because you want to be.

Client: (*sighing*) Yeah . . . we've been fighting a
                 lot. I'm feeling kind of shaky about
                 what's going to happen.

Counselor: Tell me more about that "shaky" feeling.

Client: I don't know. I love her, but I'm really
                 upset about this work thing.

Counselor: (*process*) Are you feeling shaky right now?

Client: Yes . . . I don't know what else to do to
                 make it work.

In this example, the counselor pointed out the most salient
aspect of the process: the client wasn't talking. By openly ac-
knowledging the client's discomfort, the counselor helped the
client to relax and open up.

9. Individualize your counseling.

Each counselor eventually develops a personal style of
counseling. This style may be based on a particular theoretical
approach or on experience gained in a particular work setting.
Remember that you must adapt those general rules and personal techniques for each client.

Explaining exactly *how* to individualize your counseling approach is very difficult because little consensus exists among
counselors on this subject. Counselors tend to build personal
frameworks for gauging how best to modify their counseling
approach. Some counselors assess the psychological sophistication and level of motivation of their clients; others observe social maturity and intelligence. If the client has had previous
counseling, you may be able to tailor your approach on the basis
of what worked and what didn't.

Counselors observe clients' use of language in an effort to
conduct sessions at a matching conceptual level. Be especially
careful to avoid jargon that would confuse clients.

Client: I've been really down lately—I'm getting
                 less pay because my hours at work have
                 been cut during winter. I've had to stop

	jogging, too, because of all the snow we've had.
Counselor:	You're down in the dumps.
Client:	Yeah . . . it's depressing.
Counselor:	(not) I suspect your decreased rate of receiving positive reinforcement is directly related to your depressive feelings.

Individualize you must. You may alter your language, your posture, even which counseling approach you employ. You will create a unique application of your counseling style for each client.

10. Notice resistance.

Resistance refers to an obstacle—presented by the client—that blocks the progress of counseling. Counseling theorists construe resistance differently. Psychodynamic counselors, for example, view resistance as an attempt to keep anxiety-provoking material from awareness; social learning counselors see resistance as stemming from fear of the consequences of changed behavior (Hansen, Stevic, & Warner, 1986; Shertzer & Stone, 1980). Mahoney (1987) suggests that resistance to change "is a natural expression of self-protection when core ordering processes are challenged" (p. 15). Most counseling approaches, however, acknowledge the inevitable presence of resistance.

Counselor:	Gloria, last week we agreed you would speak with your mother about some of the issues we discussed. But you haven't mentioned anything so far today about that.
Client:	Oh . . . did I say I'd speak with her? I guess I forgot.

Examples of resistance include an abrupt change of topic and forgetting important material. If the client continues to make progress despite such behavior, simply make a mental note of the resistance and go on. However, if you encounter repeated resistance, process it with the client at a time that seems right to you and at an emotional intensity that fits the client. This discussion may be all that's necessary for the client to move forward.

Client:	Oh . . . did I say I'd speak with her? I guess I forgot.
Counselor:	I know you really wanted to talk with her at the end of last week's session.
Client:	I guess I did.
Counselor:	How do you feel as we talk about it now?
Client:	Well . . . scared, really. I realized how angry she'll be if I confront her about abusing me while I was a kid.
Counselor:	You're frightened about confronting her.
Client:	Yes . . . but I want to do it. That seems like the only way for me to resolve it.

With *extreme* resistance, the counselor returns to pacing the client by decreasing the emotional intensity of the session or changing the topic (Brammer & Shostrom, 1982). In essence, the counselor gives the client permission to deal with the intense material when she or he is more able to do so.

11. When in doubt, focus on feelings.

No matter what their theoretical orientation, counselors often focus on the feelings of clients (Anton, Dunbar, & Friedman, 1976; Pope, 1979). Counselors trust clients' feelings—particularly as expressed on the nonverbal level—as indicators of salient issues.

Counselor:	I have a sense it's really important for people to like you.
Client:	(*tensing*) Yes—isn't it for everyone?

This client responded defensively, interpreting the counselor's statement to mean that such a need was abnormal or inappropriate. The counselor might follow up by asking the client what he feels when he wants people to like him.

Learning how to recognize and express feelings challenges many clients (Cormican, 1978). Clients may begin counseling unable to recognize their feelings or describe them in more than a cursory manner.

Counselor: How do you feel about losing your job?

Client: Bad. I'm very upset.

Although this client can label the intensity and direction of the feeling, descriptions like "bad/good" provide very little detail. When clients use nondescript words like "bad," "good," or "upset," ask them to elaborate. The client in this example might be feeling angry because she has to go through the job-hunting process again or sad because she believes that the job loss indicates failure on her part.

Counselors typically search for the *Big Four* of feeling words: (a) anger, (b) sadness, (c) fear, and (d) joy. An ability to recognize these feelings in clients (and to help clients become aware of them) is a sign of progress in the beginning counselor.

Counselors also attend to feelings because clients seek counseling primarily to alleviate psychological pain. Helping clients pay attention to their feelings can increase motivation to change. Fully experiencing feelings may bring insight and relief as well.

Experienced counselors can determine clients' feelings by paying attention to how *they* feel as clients talk. By sharing their reactions to clients' situations, counselors can increase clients' experience of their feelings in the here-and-now.

Client: Even though it's been a year since my father died, I still feel a hole in my life.

Counselor: As you spoke about your father I felt sad.

This technique may help a client who is having difficulty experiencing or recognizing feelings. The counselor models the feeling and reassures the client that such a feeling is okay.

A few clients see expression of feelings as an all-or-nothing proposition. These clients attest to the volcano theory of emotion: they express no affect until their feelings build up and explode.

Client: Jim, my co-worker, just kept teasing and teasing me until I couldn't stand it any more and I screamed at him.

Counselor: You were feeling very angry. How did he react when you yelled at him?

Client: He was surprised.

Assertiveness training, in which clients learn how to express feelings to others, may be appropriate for such clients (Eisler, 1976). Clients may also learn to express emotions at a moderated level by practicing such expression in counseling.

12. Plan for termination at the beginning of counseling.

Termination refers to the process that occurs at the end of counseling. At the beginning of counseling, client and counselor should reach a least a tentative understanding about when and how counseling will finish.

Counselor: When will we know counseling is complete?

Wife: When we're not fighting any more.

Husband: At least not as often as we are now, which is daily.

Counselor: If you fight only once a week, then counseling has worked.

Both: Yes.

Planning for termination means explicit goals have been set (see Cormier & Cormier, 1985, for specific information about goal setting). Goals should become clearer and may be revised (along with the termination plan) as clients move deeper into self-exploration.

Client:	I don't just want to be emotionally independent of my family—I want to have my own apartment too.
Counselor:	Moving out would signify a real step toward independence for you.
Client:	Yeah. If I did that, I'd be satisfied.

Termination should be planned, not abrupt. It is important to say good-bye, consolidate the counseling experience, discover what counseling meant to the client, and discuss future situations.

Client:	So it looks like I'm going to go to college after all.
Counselor:	I'm delighted. You worked very hard to sort things out with yourself and your family.
Client:	I certainly appreciate your help and listening to me while I was so confused about what to do.
Counselor:	Well, I enjoyed listening to you. I'm glad you're ready to go, but sad we won't be meeting any more.
Client:	Me too . . . but I know I can talk things out with my parents in the future.

Clients say good-bye in different ways (Davis, 1987). Some persons cling to the relationship and try to avoid ending; some deny any feelings; some cancel the last session. Talk with clients about how they feel about terminating. All this can be made simpler by establishing, at the onset of counseling, the conditions under which counseling will end.

Counselors often schedule several sessions to terminate. With some clients, they may schedule a monthly meeting to maintain progress.

. . . .

CHAPTER 2

Strategies to Assist Clients in Self-Exploration

This chapter provides additional guidelines for a particularly important aspect of counseling process: client self-exploration. Self-exploration refers to the elaboration and deepening of self-awareness and self-concept that occurs as clients speak about themselves. Self-exploration provides information about what must be done for change to occur and can be therapeutic in and of itself. Once clients understand what behaviors will produce desired outcomes, *some* change relatively quickly (see Butcher & Koss, 1978).

Facilitating client self-exploration depends on what you *don't do* as well as what you *do*. Beginning counselors work too hard: they feel responsible for *helping* clients, and they take that task as a mandate to give advice, ask scores of questions, and solve problems. In contrast, experienced counselors initially stay in the background and help clients thoroughly understand themselves and their problems.

13. Avoid advice.

Friends and family give advice; counselors generally don't, particularly in the initial stages of relationship building. However, many counselors (beginning and advanced) appear to believe that they must offer counsel.

Counselor: What brings you here today?

Client:	Basically, I'm having trouble with my boyfriend.
Counselor:	Have you tried talking with him?

Even though the counselor's response is a question, it implies advice (go talk with your boyfriend). Advice is an intervention and as such should be avoided until counselor and client establish a trusting relationship. However, many counselors completely avoid advice because (a) clients have already tried these simple strategies, and (b) the advice has already failed or the client wouldn't be in counseling.

Client:	I'm having trouble with my boyfriend.
Counselor:	Tell me about the trouble you are having.

It's much better strategy to encourage self-exploration, as in the example above, than to attempt premature problem solving. Because friends and family frequently offer advice to clients, your advice is likely to be old news. Also, some clients resist advice because it is externally generated; these individuals expect and want to solve their own problems.

Don't confuse giving information with giving advice (Cormier & Cormier, 1985). When you give advice, you typically provide clients with specific actions to perform. In contrast, information consists of knowledge, alternatives, or facts that clients may find useful in their decision making. As the next section explains, the usefulness of providing information also depends on when it is done.

14. Avoid premature problem solving.

Problem solving too early in counseling usually fails (see Egan, 1986). By problem solving I mean efforts by the counselor to create alternatives and suggest strategies to resolve clients' problems. Clients may resist promising solutions or already know what to do; even if clients implement a counselor's suggestion, they have only the counselor to blame or praise. Clients bear the ultimate responsibility for change. Similarly, the problems clients are facing are unlikely to be their last, and a solution selected by the counselor will not help clients learn how to handle future difficulties.

Client:	I just can't find the willpower to start studying a week before an exam.
Counselor:	Maybe if you drew up a schedule with regular study times you could study more consistently.
Client:	That would work, but I doubt that I could stick to the schedule.

Often clients know how they could obtain desired goals and outcomes but have no confidence in their personal capacity to act in the required manner. These clients lack what Bandura (1977) calls *self-efficacy*, a belief that one can perform a behavior that leads to a desired outcome. For example, alcoholic clients who have low self-efficacy for stopping drinking may relapse when they are repeatedly offered drinks at a party. Self-efficacy expectations influence whether clients initiate certain behaviors and persist in the face of obstacles.

Rather than solving problems early in counseling, counselors do better to learn what solutions have already been tried. This approach may help counselor and client to better understand why previous efforts have failed or magnified the original problem.

Counselor:	You've said that you plan to study a week before the exam, but you don't follow through. What stops you?
Client:	I start to study—I stay up all night and read, but after a couple of nights of that I just don't feel like working any more.
Counselor:	Sounds like you just get worn out.
Client:	That's right.

A client's solution to a problem can sometimes produce additional problems or exacerbate the original difficulty (Watzlawick, Weakland, & Fisch, 1974). In this example, the client became physically fatigued because of poor study habits and lost motivation to study further.

15. *Avoid relying on questions.*

Faced with their first real or role-play clients, new counselors may simply ask questions. Beginners use such questions to elicit more information or to suggest advice. It is certainly permissible to ask about specific information or to seek elaboration. However, clients may perceive a sequence of questions as threatening.

Client:	So I just left after we started to argue.
Counselor:	You were angry?
Client:	Yes.
Counselor:	Why didn't you stay and work things out?
Client:	I was too angry to talk.
Counselor:	You felt out of control?

Questions, particularly "why?" questions, put clients on the defensive and ask them to explain their behavior. Questions keep the counselor in sole control of counseling and may inappropriately lead clients. Statements that *reflect* the content or feeling clients have expressed, however, do not imply direction by the counselor.

Client:	I just left after we started to argue.
Counselor:	You got up and left the room.

Counselors also differentiate between open and closed questions (see Egan, 1986). Open questions seek elaboration by clients; closed questions ask for specific information and may be answered in a word or two. Counselors should particularly avoid sequences of closed questions when they are facilitating client self-exploration.

Client:	I just left after he started to swear at me.
Counselor:	*(open)* How did you feel then?

Client:	I was really angry. He had no right to speak to me that way—we had been close friends for years.
Counselor:	(*closed*) Did you swear back?
Client:	No.

The open-ended question in the above example encouraged the client to describe her feelings and the reason she was angry. The closed question provided no pertinent information. Unless you need very specific information, stay with open-ended inquiries.

16. Listen closely to what clients say.

As a counselor you will listen for the meaning of the words your clients use. But you can also listen for individual words and grammar. Words and the manner in which they're employed can provide important clues about how clients view the world (Bandler & Grinder, 1975).

Client:	My children always disobey me.
Counselor:	*Always?*
Client:	Well . . . not always. They usually get up and get dressed for school without any trouble.

A word like "always" indicates a distortion of reality, a predisposition to perceive different events in the same way. In the example above, the client didn't really mean "always" when he described his children's misbehavior. His recognition of this distortion of reality may help him perceive his children differently or discover a new solution.

Similarly, counselors should determine what clients mean when they use words like "must" and "should."

Client:	I *must* get an A on this test!
Counselor:	There's a feeling of desperation in your voice.
Client:	Yes. Without this grade I'm doomed.

Ellis is particularly vigilant in listening for words like "must" and "should" because he views them as signals of irrational beliefs (Ellis & Harper, 1976; Ellis & Grieger, 1977). Ellis works to detect thinking that has no basis in reality and that tends to catastrophize events.

When clients speak, they may fail to describe fully their experience (Bandler & Grinder, 1975). What is deleted or missing may be indicative of the client's problem.

Counselor:	Without an A you're doomed to what?
Client:	Well . . . I don't know. I won't maintain my 3.5 grade point average.
Counselor:	So . . .
Client:	I wouldn't get into med school.
Counselor:	And then?
Client:	Well . . . I'd be very disappointed. I guess I'd have to find another career.

Asking clients to present a fuller description of themselves is a method of facilitating self-exploration *and* helping clients change.

17. Pay attention to nonverbals.

People communicate with each other by paying attention to the verbal content of messages and to the most overt nonverbal messages (for example, smiling, frowning, making a fist). But the more subtle, nonverbal component of communication—tone of voice, facial expressions, eye contact, and body motion—conveys equally rich information. No one can tell you exactly what to look for, but the importance of observing others' nonverbals, in role plays and everyday situations, cannot be overemphasized.

One particularly effective way that counselors confront clients is to point out discrepancies between nonverbal and verbal communication.

Client:	(*smiling*) I was really upset when she said she didn't like me.

Counselor:	So you were upset . . . but I notice you were smiling when you said you were upset.
Client:	I was? Well . . . it is kind of hard for me to admit she upset me.

When faced with conflicting messages on the nonverbal and verbal levels, counselors tend to trust nonverbal communication as more indicative of basic feelings. The assumption is that it's easier to censor verbal than nonverbal communication. Counselors often help clients become aware of the nonverbal level.

Client:	(*smiling*) I was really upset when she said she didn't like me.
Counselor:	You were upset . . . but I notice you were smiling when you said you were upset.
Client:	I was? Well . . . it is kind of hard for me to admit she upset me.
Counselor:	How do you feel when you smile like that?
Client:	I don't know . . .
Counselor:	Smile again, just like you were.
Client:	(*smiling*) Okay . . .
Counselor:	How do you feel now?
Client:	Well, maybe a little safer . . . maybe you'll still like me even though she upset me.

This client was able to learn from exploration of her nonverbal movements. She learned that she smiled to hide her embarrassment about her feelings.

Counselors also express different messages on the verbal and nonverbal levels. For example, beginning counselors sometimes experience difficulty being congruent in their communication (Shertzer & Stone, 1980).

| Counselor: | (*smiling*) Your dad died two years ago today. |
| Client: | (*confused*) Yes . . . but I still feel sad about it. |

Some counselors simply feel more comfortable if they smile while around others. Such habits, however, can send mixed signals to clients. Videotaping and audiotaping sessions can help you discover any idiosyncratic nonverbal expressions that interfere with the counseling process.

18. Keep the focus on the client.

Clients often talk about other people. Others may be seen as sources of one's troubles or as standards for behavior.

| Client: | My mom thinks I should go into social work. |
| Counselor: | How do you feel about that? |

With this client, the counselor has the choice of following the other person's feelings ("What makes your mother think you should be a social worker?") or of following the client's feelings ("How do you feel about your mother's belief?"). Almost invariably, counselors return the focus to the client. The client is the focus of change in counseling, not other people. However, when others may influence the process of change, as in family or marriage counseling, counselors arrange for those relevant individuals to be present.

Many clients experience difficulty in talking about themselves. Counselors can help these clients through appropriate self-disclosures (Jourard, 1971) or self-involving responses (McCarthy & Betz, 1978; McCarthy, 1982). In self-disclosure, the counselor reveals a personal feeling or experience of his or her own; in self-involving responses, the counselor responds personally to a statement by the client. In both cases, the intent is to help clients get in touch with *their* feelings.

| Client: | So I got laid off after 15 years on the job. Now I've got to begin job hunting and I haven't the slightest idea where to start. |

Counselor: (*self-disclosing*) I know what you mean. I
                lost my last job when the agency had its
                funding cut. I was depressed.

Counselor: (*self-involving*) I feel sad that you lost
                your job.

Client: Well . . . I have been really down. I've
                been trying to think positively and ignore
                those feelings because I've got to get a job
                as soon as I can.

Self-disclosing and self-involving statements encourage
clients to reciprocate. Self-involving responses in particular may
help clients become aware of their feelings and speak more
about themselves. However, counselors' self-disclosing and
self-involving statements should be employed sparingly (to
maintain the focus on clients) and at a matching level of intensity. As an example of the latter, it would be inappropriate for a
counselor to disclose her or his current feelings of depression to
a person seeking career counseling. A more appropriate self-disclosure might involve the counselor's revelation of past feelings
of confusion and anxiety surrounding career decisions.

19. Be concrete.

Some of counseling's working materials, such as feelings
and thoughts, are intangible. For example, counselors have
compared feelings to the wind, suggesting that clients notice
emotions and allow them to pass through and change. Skilled
counselors help clients make their feelings and thoughts concrete.

Client: Even though it's been a year since Dad
                died, I still feel a hole in my life.

Counselor: Tell me about that hole.

Client: It's kind of an emptiness . . . a numbness.

Counselor: You're holding your stomach as you talk
                about the emptiness. Hold your stomach
                a minute . . . tell me what you feel.

Client:	I feel . . . sad.

Grounding feelings within the body is one method of making feelings concrete. As the example suggests, this client might learn to pay attention to his stomach whenever he feels sad. Gestalt counselors use clients' body movements, such as repeatedly making a fist or striking a pillow, to help strengthen clients' experience of feelings.

Concreteness becomes especially important when discussing clients' behavior and goals. What exactly do clients want to change? How will client and counselor know when counseling is finished?

Client:	I want to do better in school.
Counselor:	What do you mean by "better"?
Client:	I don't know . . . maybe get a 3.0 average.
Counselor:	You want a 3.0. Are you speaking about just this quarter or the whole year?
Client:	Just this quarter.

Clients sometimes have difficulty going beyond broad ideas and intellectualizations. Counselors help these clients by asking about specific events.

Client:	You know, if my husband would just complete the separation process with his family, we wouldn't argue so much.
Counselor:	Tell me an example.
Client:	Well, last week we started to argue about the phone bill, and immediately he calls his mother for advice. Then his parents are angry at me, too, and I really feel anxious.

In this example the counselor learned that the family of the client's spouse becomes inappropriately involved in their marriage. From such information the counselor might decide to pursue marriage counseling or help the client plan for such events in the future.

20. *Listen for metaphors.*

A metaphor is a figure of speech, containing an implied comparison—expressing one thing in terms of something else. Clients will occasionally offer metaphors about their issues. Listen for and accept these gifts—they are worth their weight in gold.

Client:	I'm making progress in counseling, but it sure is hard.
Counselor:	You're making a lot of effort.
Client:	Yeah . . . it reminds me of a 15-round boxing match, and we're only in round 3.

Metaphors are easy to remember. Using the boxing analogy, the counselor could ascertain the client's perception of progress in counseling (for example, round 7 would indicate further progress than round 3). Another client compared her problems to a box: the size of the box indicated the client's perception of the current intensity of her problem. When the client felt she had to place her attention elsewhere (for example, to study for a test), she "put the box in the closet for now."

21. *Summarize.*

"Summarizing" refers to a brief recapitulation of the major issues in counseling. You might summarize important issues during the counseling session, at the end of a session, or at the final counseling session. Client or counselor may summarize. Client summaries, however, present counselors with an opportunity to check their ideas about the counseling process with clients.

Counselor:	So if you were to sum up what has gone on in counseling so far, how would you describe it?

Client:	Well, I certainly understand how my parents and I get started on arguments. Everybody gets so involved in presenting their case no one listens to the other. I know I have to point that out to them, and notice it myself, or I'll get really frustrated in a hurry.
Counselor:	That certainly fits with what I've heard you say in here.

Summarizing is another method of structuring counseling. Summaries often describe important themes, keep track of change in counseling, and help interconnect related issues.

Client:	Any time I start a new class I feel really anxious. I just don't have any confidence in myself about taking risks.
Counselor:	I wonder if your lack of confidence has anything to do with your mother's over-protectiveness. You've talked about how she rarely let you try things on your own as a child. I wonder if the two are related?
Client:	That makes sense.

By summarizing a theme (the client's mother protected her from taking risks throughout childhood) that had appeared several times previously, the counselor helped the client gain insight into his current feelings of anxiety.

CHAPTER 3

. . . .

A Few Mistaken Assumptions

Counseling remains a poorly understood profession among laypersons. Many people still see counseling, for example, as a place only for the sick, weak, or severely disturbed. Beginning counselors must *unlearn* some of the common assumptions they bring with them to training. In a sense, this book is a role induction for beginning counselors and a role reminder for experienced therapists.

1. Positive thinking does not equal rational thinking.

Some beginning counselors mistakenly equate Ellis's concepts of rational and irrational thinking with positive and negative thinking. Positive and negative thinking usually refer to beliefs that one will encounter good or bad fortune. Irrational thinking refers to a belief, unsupported by objective evidence, that leads to a painful feeling (Ellis & Grieger, 1977).

Client: I *must* get an A on all of my final exams or I'm doomed.

Counselor: You're saying you must be perfect in all of your classes.

As I noted in the preceding chapter, words like "must" indicate irrational beliefs. In this case, the counselor interpreted the client's obsession with perfect grades as the irrational belief.

Whereas counselors may help clients improve their self-esteem and self-confidence, they avoid trying to talk clients into improvement. Particularly with persons whose problems are long-standing, verbal persuasion, by itself, is one of the weakest methods of promoting change (Bandura, 1977).

Client:	For years I've been afraid people will laugh at me if I speak in class.
Counselor:	(*ill-advised*) You just have to believe people are going to like you.
Client:	I know that, but I can't do it.

Instead, counselors challenge clients to provide proof that their catastrophic beliefs will come true. Frequently counselors work with clients to design homework to test the rationality of their beliefs.

Client:	I'm afraid people will laugh at me if I speak in class.
Counselor:	What could you do to test that belief?
Client:	Well . . . I could ask a question.
Counselor:	That makes sense to me. How about asking one question in each of your classes and seeing how people respond?

At the following session, counselor and client would discuss the results of the homework. In this example, the client would likely learn that no one laughed at her questions. Even if a classmate later ridiculed the student, the counselor might acknowledge the unpleasantness of that event but point out that the student did survive it without any real catastrophic outcomes.

2. Agreement does not equal empathy.

Some beginning counselors interpret empathy to mean agreement or sympathy. Empathy refers to the comprehension of the subjective world of the client (see Egan, 1986). Agreement suggests that the counselor approves of the client's behavior, while "sympathy" indicates that the counselor feels sorry for the client.

Client:	I was really angry when he said to go home.
Counselor:	(*empathy*) You felt angry with him.
Counselor:	(*agreement*) Good for you. I'm glad you left!
Counselor:	(*sympathy*) He is awfully mean to you!

Friends and family provide agreement and sympathy. Counselors provide empathy to help clients explore their problems and become aware of their feelings and thoughts. In that way clients begin to understand what they should do to change.

3. Do not assume that change is simple.

Clients typically expect to change some aspect of their lives so they will feel better. However, matters are seldom so simple. Human behavior has multiple causes, and no counselor can always be aware of all the factors helping and hindering change. Such factors as significant others, biological influences, and individual differences in response to therapy can all contribute to the complexity of the counseling process.

Client:	I started on the homework, but mother says she doesn't think it will work. She says I should stop counseling.
Counselor:	(*surprised*) Well . . . that's the first I've heard about your mother since our first session.
Client:	I think she might be right.

The counselor had been proceeding on the assumption that changes in the client's behavior would resolve the presenting problem. However, the client's mother has intervened and may now need to be included in the counseling process.

Counselors sometimes do marriage and family therapy because they view individuals' problems as relating to the social systems to which they belong (deShazer, 1982; Minuchin, 1974). Change is not simply a matter of altering the "misbehaving" person. An adolescent may act out at school to *stabilize* her family system: her feuding parents, considering divorce, might table their disagreements to handle the current crisis. More effective counseling would focus on the entire family instead of just the identified client.

4. Make psychological assessments, not moral judgments.

One of the most difficult tendencies to alter, in some beginners, is judging people. Being judgmental involves moral or ethical assessments.

Client: So I began to drink again after I lost my job.

Counselor: You really let your family down there, didn't you?

Instead of judging whether behavior is right or wrong, counselors assess clients in terms of psychological theory and practice. Such assessments might inquire into family background, educational and employment experience, psychopathology, intellectual abilities, or strengths. What you assess depends on what you believe to influence behavior and progress in counseling. Your beliefs about assessment, in turn, should be based on your counseling experience, as well as on relevant theory and research.

Client: So I began to drink again after I lost my job. I sat at home a lot, and I just kept getting more irritable.

Counselor: It sounds like you felt very stressed and then started to drink again.

In this example the counselor suggests a psychological cause for the client's drinking, a cause that the client can influence and for which the client bears responsibility. No condemnation of the person is involved, however.

Sin and forgiveness are religious terms, not counseling concepts. Many clergy perform pastoral counseling in which they serve not as preachers but as skilled listeners and helpers. Some beginning counselors, however, view counseling as a means of promoting religious values to solve clients' problems. Although it has well-intentioned and skilled followers, religious counseling is a contradiction in terms if practitioners intend, through their counseling, to save or convert their clients. Clients have a right to their personal values.

5. Do not assume that you know clients' feelings, thoughts, and behaviors.

When we talk with other people, ordinarily we assume we know what they are feeling or thinking. Experience in counseling demonstrates the fallacy of this assumption.

Client: So I just left after we started to argue.

Counselor: You were very angry.

Client: No, I had to leave for work in ten minutes and I knew we'd never resolve anything in that amount of time.

In this example the client corrected the counselor's misperception. In practice, many clients will tell you when you are wrong. Listen for these corrections.

To avoid the feeling that they know everything, counselors proceed with a sense of tentativeness (Egan, 1986). They act as though they might have misunderstood, and they ask their clients for confirmation of what they know. They verify their assumptions about clients' feelings, thoughts, and behaviors.

Counselor: You seem sad as you speak of your father. Is that how you feel?

Client: No, I didn't feel sad as much as I felt angry about getting into another argument.

Counselors express their tentativeness in this form: a reflection of feeling or content followed by a question. Even if the counselor's reflection misses, clients will respond with further elaboration.

Tentativeness reminds counselors of their ignorance of clients' subjective worlds, and it also provides room to make mistakes. Beginning counselors sometimes feel they cannot err. If you believe, for example, that you can seriously damage a client with a single statement, you hold to what Meehl (1973) called "the spun-glass theory of the mind." Although counseling can be harmful, clients are not so fragile as to be psychologically destroyed by a single statement. If you pace and lead skillfully, you will sense the effects of counseling on clients and adjust accordingly.

6. Do not assume that you know how clients react to their feelings, thoughts, and behaviors.

Clients differ in their perceptions and reactions to the events in their lives and even to their psychological states. For example, one client may panic when he begins to feel depressed, believing this to be the first sign of mental illness; another may accept depression simply as a sign of physical and emotional fatigue. Be wary of assuming that how *you* respond to an event or feeling corresponds to how your *client* reacts.

Observe how clients react to their psychological states. Clients sometimes create additional problems by how they perceive the original difficulty.

Counselor:	So you feel angry toward your son when he deliberately disobeys you.
Client:	(*tentatively*) Yes.
Counselor:	I sense you're uncomfortable with that anger.
Client:	I get scared whenever I get mad at him. Good mothers don't get angry.

This client was troubled both by her son *and* by her anger toward him. What sometimes frightens clients about their feelings is the belief that they must *act* on every feeling. For example, if parents feel angry toward their children, they may feel like hitting the children. Typically, parents may then reject the behavior (hitting) *and* the feeling (rage, anger). Clients can learn that it is acceptable to experience any feeling; however, one should not act upon every feeling. Feelings are indicators of our psychological states, not sole determinants of our behavior. We have choices.

Other clients may be afraid of or confused by their feelings. For example, persons mourning the death of a loved one may be surprised by the type and intensity of their emotions.

Client:	I'm just beginning to realize how much I hated my father. But I always thought I loved him!
Counselor:	You're starting to feel angry about his abuse of you as a child.
Client:	I think I'm going crazy!

Reassurance helps with such clients, as does group counseling with others having similar experiences.

Client 1:	This is hard for me to admit . . . but I've had really negative feelings about my father since he died.
Client 2:	What kind of feelings?
Client 1:	Well . . . anger, mostly.
Client 2:	I probably felt most angry with my father right after he died.
Client 1:	(*surprised*) Really?
Client 2:	Yeah . . . I don't think that's unusual at all. I know a lot of people who had to deal with that anger.

Client 1 learned that sadness is not the only feeling people can experience when someone close dies.

In sum, clients' appraisals of thoughts and feelings may result in even more intense problems (such as panic attacks) should those appraisals indicate that their feelings are wrong, are inappropriate, or fall short of imaginary standards. Help clients learn how they react to themselves.

CHAPTER 4

. . . .

Special Issues

In this chapter I address important differences in counseling process and client characteristics, as well as several pragmatic aspects of counseling. For many clients, the counseling process is not a matter of meeting weekly for weeks or months; crises often bring clients into counseling, and in these instances change must occur quickly. Variability is also present in client characteristics. Kiesler (1971) developed the term *uniformity myth* to describe the belief that all clients are basically alike. Clients are different, and in this chapter I cover some of the potentially important differences, such as gender and race. Finally, I'll briefly discuss practical issues such as the arrangement of the counseling setting, documenting counseling progress in writing, and the referral process.

1. Develop crisis intervention skills.

Because of the stigma sometimes associated with counseling ("Only sick people see counselors"), it may take a crisis to motivate some to seek therapy. Crises occur when individuals are faced with overwhelming problems they feel they cannot handle (Caplan, 1961; Puryear, 1979; Slaikeu, 1984). A person in crisis could be someone who has been depressed for a long period or a person experiencing an acute psychotic episode. Counselors agree about basic steps for working with crisis clients. These actions differ from counselors' normal behaviors in the initial stage of counseling.

For many beginning counselors, the most frightening type of client in crisis is a person considering suicide. First, follow up on any mention of suicide or indication that clients have thought about harming themselves. Don't worry that you will be giving clients a new idea if you ask about suicide. Clients may feel relieved when asked because suicide is so difficult to discuss with friends and family.

Client: I've been depressed for so long now that I've just about given up hope. I don't see any way out.

Counselor: You seem so hopeless that I wonder if you have thought about hurting yourself.

A client might respond like this:

Client: Oh, no, I'd never do that. But I might have to move the family away from here to look for work.

Some clients, however, have considered suicide. Counselors then determine *lethality*—that is, how likely these clients are to attempt suicide (for a more complete discussion, see Slaikeu, 1984, pp. 94-101).

Client: Yes . . . I just want to die.

Counselor: Have you thought about a way to kill yourself?

Client: Yes . . .

Counselor: Please tell me about it.

Client: I have an empty gun in my bedroom drawer.

Counselor: You've had serious thoughts about doing this. Have you been thinking about buying bullets?

Client: No, not really. I just feel like I want the gun around.

The first question to ask, then, is: *Does the client have a method in mind?* The more specific and concrete the method, the greater the likelihood the client will attempt suicide. Without knowing more than the information contained in the above example, I would estimate this client's lethality risk as moderate to high. A method is available, but additional action is necessary before suicide would be imminent. The second question should elicit information about the existence and nature of previous suicide attempts.

Counselor: You have a gun, but no bullets. Have you tried to commit suicide before?

Client: Yes. I tried to slash my wrists. My wife found me and they rushed me to the emergency room.

The second question, then, is: *Have you previously attempted suicide?* The client in the above example indicated that he had made a previous attempt and that it had been a serious attempt. Predicting suicide, like predicting other outcomes in counseling, is problematic. However, the information about a previous serious attempt, combined with an available method, would increase the assessment of the client's lethality to serious. In such a case, counselors ethically and legally have a responsibility to take action to preserve a client's life. This action ranges from further immediate counseling to voluntary or involuntary hospitalization of the client. Beginning counselors should learn how to assess for lethality and know what local procedures are employed with suicidal clients. Beginning counselors should *always* consult with supervisors if suicide is a possibility.

Even when suicide is unlikely, counselors working with clients in crisis take more action than they normally do. Such directiveness is embodied in the following crisis intervention strategies.

(a) Take control of the situation.

Particularly with suicidal clients, counselors must take direct action. In crises, most clients have given up control or perceive a great loss of control. The counselor should restore order and predictability. In other words, the counselor takes the lead.

Client: (*angrily*) Everyone here hates me! I won't leave my room. I'm not going to eat or sleep or do anything but JUST SIT HERE!

Counselor 1:	Tony, I understand you feel you've come to the end of your rope. But you've been sitting on your bed for two days and we can't leave until we can find a way to help you.
Client:	No one else will talk to me. Why should you?
Counselor 2:	I care about what happens to you. Bill and I are from the community mental health center and we'd like to listen to what's bothering you....

It's worth noting that in this example two counselors worked as a crisis intervention team. Teams of counselors (or of counselors combined with other professionals, such as nurses and police officers) often work as crisis interventionists. A team effort decreases the stress on individual counselors and increases the potential resources available to help the client.

(b) Determine who is the real client.

In crisis situations, the identified client may not be the real client—that is, the person who needs attention. Each crisis situation always contains an identified client who, for example, may be threatening suicide or homicide. Identified clients, however, may be calm and clear about what they want, whereas persons dealing with the identified client may be quite anxious and uncertain.

Puryear (1979) describes a crisis he encountered as a counselor in the army. He received a 2 a.m. phone call at home from the emergency room nurse, who anxiously informed him that the emergency room doctor wanted him to come to the hospital immediately. At first, the nurse would not tell Puryear why he should come to the hospital other than to say, "Dr. Smith wants you to come in now." Finally, the nurse whispered that a patient had a gun. Puryear asked that the patient be put on the telephone, learned that the patient wanted to be admitted to the psychiatric ward, and agreed to authorize his admission if the patient gave the gun to the doctor. The patient gave up the gun and Puryear authorized the admission. That resolved the crisis.

In this example, the emergency room doctor and nurse clearly were under a great deal of stress. Nurses, medical doctors, police officers, and other helping professionals with little mental health experience sometimes become apprehensive when dealing with a crisis client. Your job as a crisis counselor, then, is to assess *all* the people involved in the crisis situation. Treat everyone with respect, but don't accept information and commands at face value. Work with everyone who is in crisis; in practical terms, this may mean that you will counsel the helping professional who has requested your assistance. Stay in control and avoid getting caught up in others' feelings of panic.

(c) Emphasize the positive.

Emphasize strengths as a way of helping clients regain control in a crisis (see Puryear, 1979, pp. 86-104, for a more complete discussion). Even a relatively minor strength or act can be noted.

Client:	What can I do? I'm a jerk. I'm flunking four classes and nobody will talk to me.
Counselor:	Hmmm.
Client:	I can't do anything!
Counselor:	Well, you can sit in one place for two days and not eat anything. That's a pretty difficult thing to do.
Client:	Well . . . that's true.
Counselor:	Maybe you could use that toughness in some other ways.
Client:	I don't know.
Counselor:	Well, let's keep talking. But remember that toughness. It could be a big help.
Client:	Okay.

Note the extent to which clients accept your positive attributions about them. Crisis counselors take control of crisis situations, but they give that control back at a rate consonant with the client's emotional state.

(d) Mobilize social resources.

Find and mobilize clients' social support networks. Determine whether friends and family are available to stay with crisis clients.

Counselor: Juan, I haven't heard you mention your family in any of this.

Client: My parents don't care and neither do any of my brothers or sisters . . . except Chris. And she's in Colorado.

Counselor: Tell me about Chris.

Client: She's the person in the family I talk with the most. She convinced me to come to college because I did well in high school.

Counselor: Don't you think she might be concerned about you now, given how you feel?

Client: I don't know.

Counselor: What would you do if she felt depressed?

Client: Well . . . I'd go visit her . . . maybe I could call her.

Arranging for a crisis client to stay with family and friends provides emotional stability. Once an equilibrium has been reestablished, discuss ways the client could seek further help. If possible, schedule an appointment with a counselor.

Crisis intervention provides good experience for beginning counselors. You quickly build confidence and knowledge. Client change occurs more rapidly than it does in normal circumstances, and the difficulty level and content of crisis counseling varies greatly. At the same time, continued crisis work over an extended period can be stressful and draining to counselors (see Freudenberger, 1974). As a preventive act, many agencies rotate counselors in and out of crisis work to provide periods of less intensive effort.

2. Pay attention to gender and racial/ethnic issues.

Counselors strive to value equality between men and women while trying to understand how sources of inequality affect them (Richardson & Johnson, 1984). Although women make up the majority of clients, only recently has attention turned to gender issues in counseling. At a minimum, female clients should receive sex-fair counseling; that is, they should receive the same type of counseling as males (Helms, 1979). Specifically, counselors should avoid fostering traditional sex roles, devaluing women, or responding to women as sex objects (see Gilbert & Waldroop, 1978).

Career counselors should be especially sensitive to gender issues (see Betz & Hackett, 1981). Women should not be directed away from considering specific occupations because of the counselor's sex-role stereotypes (Abramowitz, Weitz, Schwartz, Amura, Gomes, & Abramowitz, 1975). Other reasons women have been turned away from rewarding occupations include social pressure and inappropriately low self-estimates of ability.

Counselor:	Barbara, I see that your vocational interest scores suggest that a career in engineering is a possibility.
Female Client:	I've always liked my math courses, but . . . I doubt I have the ability to be an engineer.
Counselor:	What is it you don't think you can do?
Client:	I don't know . . . I just can't see myself working as an engineer.

Evidence suggests that women tend to discount success and underestimate their abilities for some types of tasks (see Dweck, 1986). Counselors have a responsibility to help their clients make decisions based on accurate information and sound judgment.

| Counselor: | Barbara, you seem very doubtful of your ability in mathematics. |

Client:	I am. I *like* math—I've always gotten A's—but I don't know about being an engineer. I mean, I've never even heard of a woman engineer.
Counselor:	You're right—there aren't that many female engineers compared to males. But that has more to do with stereotypes than ability.
Client:	I guess it's worth taking a look at. Does the school's internship program have an engineering placement?
Counselor:	Yes. You could spend part of this summer working part time for an engineering company. It might give you a more realistic idea of what engineers do—and what obstacles you'll face.
Client:	It's worth a try.

Counselors also need to be aware of sexism in our culture (Richardson & Johnson, 1984). Sexism refers to discrimination on the basis of gender. Examples include lower pay for women who work the same jobs as men, sexual harassment at work, and different standards for judging mental health in women and men. Counselors' responses to sexism range from helping clients become aware of how gender issues affect their lives to promoting social change.

Like gender, racial and ethnic issues have been relatively neglected in counseling and psychology until recently (Casas, 1984). Counselors strive to understand clients' behavior in the context of their cultural background (Sue, 1978). They attend to the strengths present in minority clients as well as the difficulties resulting from living in the majority-group culture.

Counselors should pay attention to their old stereotypes and biases about people different from themselves. Such misconceptions can inappropriately change the counseling process. For example, on the basis of race you might alter your idea of what constitutes healthy behavior, or on the basis of gender you might change your judgment about the appropriateness of intensely expressed emotion.

Although research in the area is controversial (see Casas, 1984), some agencies match counselors and clients by race, hoping this assignment facilitates counseling progress (Pope, 1979; Russell, 1970, cited in Shertzer & Stone, 1980). In general, the greater the similarity between counselor and client (in terms of race, sex, culture, etc.), the more easily a therapeutic relationship will develop.

However, generalizations about minority group status or gender should be applied cautiously to counseling practice because of the large individual differences that exist within these groups.

3. Be open to group and family approaches.

Many counselors see one-to-one counseling as the treatment of choice for all clients. However, clinical experience and some research suggests that substantial advantages exist for group and family approaches (see Yalom, 1985; Bednar & Kaul, 1978; Gurman & Kniskern, 1978).

Particularly from an administrative point of view, groups are very efficient. If one counselor can work with ten clients in one ninety-minute session, that represents considerable savings in comparison to one counselor working ten one-hour sessions. From a client's perspective, groups provide emotional support, models of coping behavior, and evidence that one's problems are shared by others (for elaboration of these and other advantages of groups, see Yalom, 1985; Schneider Corey & Corey, 1987).

Selecting clients by similar age or social maturity can produce a homogeneous group that grows in cohesion and helpfulness (Shertzer & Stone, 1980). Members of helpful groups feel part of the group as a whole and benefit from the open giving and receiving of feelings and ideas (see Schneider Corey & Corey, 1987; Barrett-Lennard, 1974).

Client 1:	I want to be an engineer, but I really don't know if I can do it.
Client 2:	I felt the same way last year. People thought I was odd because I didn't want to be a secretary.
Client 1:	That's right. That's what my parents say.

Counselors normally select clients for groups through individual interviews. By this means they can determine if clients possess sufficient social skills and emotional stability to benefit from a group. In family therapy, counselors often employ a systems approach. Family therapists see individuals' problems as relating to the social systems to which they belong, the most important of which is the family (deShazer, 1982; Minuchin, 1974). Families often act to preserve their status quo; in some families this means that members act to keep certain individuals "sick." The first task of the family counselor, then, is to observe the communication patterns of family members (see Satir, 1972). Next, the counselor points out the maladaptive interactions and helps the family members change so that they can build a new structure of communication and interaction.

4. Refer carefully.

You cannot help every client. You may lack the necessary skills; clients may move out of the area; you and a particular client may simply be unable to work together. Regardless of the reason, you should be aware of other resources in the community.

Client: We're moving to Seattle in a month, but I'd still like to continue therapy with someone.

Counselor: Actually, I know several counselors in that area who work as private practitioners. I can give you their names and phone numbers if you like.

Client: That would help. Would you be willing to speak to my new counselor if that's necessary?

Counselor: Yes. You should sign a release-of-information form so I can do that.

To respect clients' rights and to ensure that they follow through, explain the reason when you make a referral. After your explanation, seek a reaction to your referral.

Counselor:	I think a psychological test might save time and help me get a better sense of what is happening with you.
Client:	What kind of test?
Counselor:	It's called the Minnesota Multiphasic Personality Inventory, or MMPI. It takes about an hour and a half, and it will help us decide what direction to go in counseling. What do you think?
Client:	That's okay. I think maybe I took that test a few years ago at the school I transferred from.
Counselor:	Okay. We have to set up an appointment for you at the testing center. Maybe we can also track down those previous results—with your permission.

If you have questions about *whether* or *to whom* to refer, consult with colleagues and supervisors.

5. Watch for deterioration in clients.

Counselors rarely consider that they may harm their clients. But considerable evidence exists to suggest that some clients deteriorate in counseling (Bergin & Lambert, 1978).

In research on groups, Lieberman, Yalom, and Miles (1973) found that leaders who were frequently aggressive, authoritarian, and inappropriately self-disclosing produced the greatest number of dropouts and negative changers (people who became worse after counseling). Stuart (1974) attempted to educate 935 students in the seventh and ninth grades through 10 classroom sessions about drugs. These students reported significant increases in their knowledge about drugs—and in their use of alcohol, marijuana, and LSD.

No generic prescriptions can be given for avoiding negative change in counseling. However, you should assess and observe client reaction to every intervention. The following interaction, for example, might occur in the beginning stages of counseling.

Client:	I have faint recollections about my father hurting me when I was very young....
Counselor:	Did your father abuse you?
Client:	I... I don't know. I'm starting to get very upset.
Counselor:	You seem anxious....
Client:	Yes. I'm very scared.
Counselor:	How do you feel about talking about this?
Client:	I'm not ready. Not yet... at least not this fast.
Counselor:	That's okay. We'll come back to this later.

In this example the counselor assessed the client's feelings about further probing of the potential abuse. Since the counseling process was still in the early stages, the counselor decided to table the probe and reapproach the issue later in counseling.

Pushing clients too fast may be harmful. Counseling approaches like Gestalt emphasize frustrating and confronting clients. Gestalt counselors, however, still observe their clients to determine the effects of confrontation.

6. Establish an interest in counseling research.

Counseling is an art in the throes of becoming a science. At present, practitioners can do more than researchers can explain. For example, counselors can help clients with phobias and depression, but researchers can only partially explain the etiology of those problems and why counseling works with them when it does. A substantial split currently separates practitioners and researchers: researchers dismiss practitioners as "touchy-feely," while practitioners view current research as irrelevant (Gelso, 1979; Meehl, 1956). However, practitioner-scientists, theoreticians, and other researchers are the groups likely to discover the patterns and order that occur in effective counseling and psychotherapy.

Competent counselors and psychotherapists should understand the research process, if not contribute to it. Keep up with
current research by reading such journals as these:

Journal of Consulting and Clinical Psychology
Journal of Counseling Psychology
Professional Psychology: Research and Practice
Journal of Counseling and Development
Behavior Therapy
Cognitive Therapy and Research
Clinical Psychology Review
Psychotherapy: Theory, Research and Practice
American Journal of Psychiatry

Counselors who understand the research process are better
able to conduct, cooperate with, and coordinate research in applied settings (such as hospitals, clinics, college counseling
centers, and community mental health centers). Applied settings, because of their primary orientation to service, typically
present counseling researchers with substantial obstacles to establishing and maintaining research, be it single case designs or
large outcome studies. Conducting research in field settings,
however, provides an excellent source of research questions and
offers great potential for producing results relevant to actual
clients and problems.

Beginning counselors who desire to learn about research
should ally themselves with a faculty member or counselor conducting empirical work (Gelso, 1979). Such an alliance teaches
the beginner research skills and demonstrates the day-to-day
difficulties of conducting counseling research. Researchers in
applied settings must learn, for example, how to protect their
scarce research time against service demands and how to handle the politics of conducting research in a service agency
(Gelso, 1979).

7. Document your work.

After each counseling session, take notes. Documentation
has four benefits: (a) records provide support for you in any

legal action; (b) records allow you to accurately inform your supervisor of progress and issues; (c) records enable you to comply with agency standards for accountability (such as the number of hours spent in individual counseling or issues to be addressed should a client terminate and later return for further counseling); (d) records remind you of treatment history and amount of progress.

What should you write in your notes? This depends partially on where you work, but in general you should, for each session, briefly describe: (a) principal content and themes; (b) noteworthy counselor interventions, with client response; (c) client status (including descriptions of client cognitions, affect, and behavior); (d) expected client behavior during the period leading up to the next session, including any homework; (e) expected time and interventions still required to meet counseling goals; and (f) indications of client expectations for outcome of counseling. Your notes could also include tests administered (with results and client reactions), diagnoses, your reaction to the session, questions to ask supervisors or colleagues, and relevant client interactions with family and friends.

Such notes should be kept under lock and key where no one may access them purposefully or by accident. Computerized record-keeping systems are also available (see programs from Applied Innovations, 1985, or Instructional Enterprises, 1984).

8. Persevere with no-shows.

Beginning counselors sometimes have difficulty knowing how to react when their clients fail to attend scheduled sessions. One student's first three clients didn't show up, and the student assumed that something was wrong with his initial phone contact to make appointments. Another counselor became angry with a client for failing to attend a session; he subsequently decided not to attend the next session, rationalizing that he wasn't certain the client was going to attend. The client did.

Avoid judgments on no-shows. At the next contact (a follow-up phone call or scheduled session), ask the client about the nonattendance. Determine if the failure to attend reflects on progress (or lack thereof) in counseling or the client's characteristic manner of dealing with people. In essence, regard no-shows as material for therapy rather than as a personal affront.

Counselor:	Amy, you missed the last two sessions.
Client:	Yeah. I just didn't feel like coming.
Counselor:	Tell me more.
Client:	After our last session I felt so depressed I didn't want to talk about my problems any more.

No-shows become especially complicated when clients interpret them as additional failures. For example, clients may skip an appointment after a particularly difficult session. However, they may then see the no-show as an indication that they are unable or unworthy to continue counseling. Premature termination becomes a real possibility. You might avoid this failure loop by giving such clients excused absences—that is, planned permission to miss a session. This arrangement may increase some clients' willingness to attend future meetings following a no-show.

Client:	I missed the first session because I didn't feel like talking. And then I got embarrassed because I didn't show up.
Counselor:	So you missed the second session because of your embarrassment. Why don't we just agree it's okay for you to miss a session if you call ahead and cancel?
Client:	Gee . . . that sounds okay.

If *you* must cancel a session, inform the client as soon as possible and reschedule.

9. Arrange the physical setting appropriately.

The counseling process is affected by the physical characteristics of the counselor and the counseling setting (Davis, 1987; see Langs, 1973, for a more complete treatment).

(a) Dress appropriately.

Dressing for success may be more necessary in business than in counseling, but some clients judge counselors by their attire. A conservative appearance that matches that of other colleagues is fitting. Dress becomes problematic when counselors draw attention to themselves through apparel.

(b) Don't sit behind a desk.

Face the client with no physical objects between you. Clients may interpret partial concealment as inaccessibility. If possible, provide comfortable chairs for counselor and client. This makes it easier for both to concentrate during the entire length of the session.

(c) Conduct counseling in a quiet setting.

If you can overhear another conversation during a counseling session, it's likely that someone can overhear your (confidential?) discussion. Respecting clients' privacy and confidentiality means counseling should occur in a quiet, private setting.

(d) Avoid interruptions and distractions.

Don't accept phone calls; don't read the mail; don't finish your lunch. Attention in a counseling session belongs exclusively to the client, except in the case of an emergency.

(e) Be prompt.

If clients arrive late or leave early, that's an issue to address in counseling. In any event, clients should not be wondering about the whereabouts of their counselors ten minutes after the scheduled start. A regularity to the beginning and end of counseling sessions signals that clients can trust this relationship. Similarly, arranging the session for the same time each week or day can signify the counselor's commitment to the relationship.

Some clients measure their importance to the counselor by how often their sessions exceed the scheduled time. Be explicit with clients about the length of a session. A typical individual counseling session lasts 45 or 50 minutes. This is enough time to go beyond the superficial, but not so long that client and counselor are exhausted.

(f) Invest in a box of tissues.

Sometimes clients cry.

(g) Restrict your communications about clients to professional colleagues in professional settings.

Counselors may be tempted to discuss clients in public places such as restaurants and buses. Particularly in small towns and other settings where people who overhear those conversations might know the individuals involved, talking about clients in public has the potential for *big* trouble. Restrict your discussion of clients to supervisors and necessary colleagues in work settings.

CHAPTER 5

Counselor, Know Thyself

In no other profession does the personality and behavior of the professional make such a difference as it does in counseling. Beginning counselors work at increasing their self-awareness as well as their knowledge of counseling procedures. Your willingness to be open to supervision, to accept clients' failures and criticisms, and to acknowledge your limits will contribute to your eventual success and satisfaction as a counselor.

1. Become aware of your personal issues.

Every beginning counselor will eventually confront difficult questions about her or his personal issues. Answers to these questions may not be readily apparent. Your issues, however, do influence how you counsel (see Egan, 1986).

Experience in counseling, competent supervision, and the development of a personal theory of counseling will help you answer the questions that follow.

(a) How did you decide to become a counselor?

Many counselors became interested in a helping profession because family and friends sought them out to listen and provide help. Other counselors were once clients themselves and decided to follow in the footsteps of counselors who helped them.

Your reasons for becoming a counselor may affect how you counsel. For example, did your assistance to friends include acting as a rescuer? Rescuers are persons who do the problem solving and helping in their social groups. As a counselor, will you again rescue?

Client: I just don't have the willpower to eat more.

Counselor: You can call me any time of the day or night when you need help.

Can you allow clients to handle their own problems?

Client: I just don't have as much willpower as I once had.

Counselor: What stops you from using the willpower you do possess?

A counselor may solve a problem for a client. A counselor may also help clients learn how to solve problems successfully. The difference is important.

(b)   With what emotions are you uncomfortable?

Clients often experience intense feelings such as rage or grief. Because of their lack of exposure, beginning counselors may be uncomfortable with some feelings, at least at the intensity level expressed by clients. Will you allow clients to express those emotions? Are there feelings you avoid, that you will steer your clients away from?

Client: I just hurt so much since the divorce.

Counselor: Try not to think about it. Are you having any luck getting dates?

In this example the counselor unconsciously moved the discussion away from the intense hurt. Counselor training includes exposure and desensitization to a range and intensity of feelings new to beginning counselors. Identify the issues that make you uncomfortable. For example, as a new counselor I was afraid of talking with clients about their sexuality (particularly homosexuality), their feelings of rage, and their feelings of helplessness. Without help from supervisors and the experience of personal counseling, I would have continued to avoid those areas when my clients ventured near them.

(c) What amount of progress is acceptable?

Although individuals differ in the progress they make in counseling, beginning counselors are sometimes surprised at how slowly clients change. Most clients cannot alter their troublesome behavior quickly or at the instruction of the counselor. For counselors, the issue becomes how much progress is acceptable.

Client:	I know I agreed to speak in each of my classes, but . . .
Counselor:	(silence)
Client:	. . . but I only asked one question, in physics.

What will be a blow to your confidence as a counselor? A client who drops out? Ask yourself what rewards you expect as a counselor. Do you want money, status in the community, or intimacy without threat?

(d) How will you deal with your clients' feelings for you?

If the counseling relationship becomes at all significant to the client, she or he will have feelings for you. Interestingly, these feelings may have little to do with what you've said or done. Clients may transfer feelings from past relationships onto their perceptions of you. Clients' feelings about their counselors are generally referred to as *transference* (see Hansen, Stevic, & Warner, 1986, or Shertzer & Stone, 1980, for a general introduction; see Robertiello & Schoenewolf, 1987, for advanced examples).

How will you feel if a client perceives you as attractive, wise, or racist?

Client:	I know you don't like me.
Counselor:	What makes you say that?
Client:	You don't like me because I'm blind!

In general, counselors process such feelings with their clients. Because this processing may influence progress, it is im-

portant to develop your ability to recognize and work with
clients' feelings for you.

(e) How will you handle your feelings for your clients?

You may have strong or ambivalent feelings about clients.
Counselors' feelings about their clients are generally referred to
as *countertransference* (again, see Hansen, Stevic, & Warner, 1986;
Shertzer & Stone, 1980; Robertiello & Schoenewolf, 1987). Is it
okay for you to feel sexually attracted to a client? What will you
do with that feeling? Perhaps you came from a family where
you were abused as a child. Will you be able to work with child
abusers? You too may transfer your feelings about past relationships onto your clients.

Client:	I've always gotten my way. I was always the biggest kid in grade school, and I just bullied anybody who got in my way.
Counselor:	*(angrily)* Don't you think you were a jerk to do that?

Counselors-in-training (and professional counselors, for
that matter) often engage in their own therapy both for personal
growth and to be better able to help their clients.

Client:	I've always gotten my way. I was always the biggest kid in grade school, and I just bullied anybody who got in my way.
Counselor:	Anyone who gets in your way gets pushed aside.
Client:	Yeah ... but bullying doesn't always get me what I want with my family and co-workers.

The relationship between counselor and client sometimes
parallels other relationships. For example, if sarcasm is part of
a client's interpersonal style, sarcasm is likely to be part of the
client's verbal behavior with the counselor. Similarly, the feelings that the client engenders in you, the counselor, may be experienced by others as well. Some counselors judge progress in
counseling (particularly for clients with interpersonal difficul-

ties) by changes in the relationship between counselor and client.

Counselor: You know, Lars, I sense that you've felt more relaxed talking with me the past couple of weeks.

Client: I guess I don't feel quite as suspicious of people as I used to. Funny—a friend of mine said the same thing last week.

In this example the counselor noticed less tension in the relationship. The client acknowledged a change in his interpersonal style both in and out of counseling.

(f) Can you be flexible, accepting, and gentle?

The attitudes you hold toward counseling and clients affect the process and outcome of counseling. Flexibility refers to the counselor's ability to be creative, open, and aware of the here-and-now in counseling (Van Kaam, 1966, cited in Hansen, Stevic, & Warner, 1986). Acceptance is the counselor's willingness to hear and understand whatever the client says without judgment, without conditions. Gentleness is the capacity to be kind and considerate even when clients are abrupt, afraid, and defensive.

Client: You're not helping me. I can't talk about this!

Counselor: *(softly)* How difficult it is for you to remember your childhood. . . .

Client: It hurts so much.

Counselor: *(silence)*

As a profession, counselors and therapists are probably more accepting of individual differences than any other group. Such tolerance can be learned.

2. Be open to supervision.

The set of questions we've just discussed may be overwhelming to beginners wondering how they will ever become. so self-aware. Relax—counselors are not expected to be self-actualized. You are expected, however, to know the areas where you have personal difficulties. Counseling involves knowing yourself, not just techniques and theory; in this area, a competent supervisor can be invaluable. Supervision is more than instruction, consultation, or direction (see Whiteley, 1982; Bartlett, Goodyear, & Bradley, 1983). Supervision resembles counseling when it involves exploring the supervisee's personal issues.

Counselor: So when he started to talk about dying, I really became anxious. I started to sweat and feel really dizzy.

Supervisor: What was it that frightened you?

Counselor: I don't know. . . .

Supervisor: It was when he mentioned dying that you became anxious.

Counselor: I just haven't dealt with death much, and he was feeling so afraid. That triggered the same feelings in me.

Supervision is the best setting in which to explore feelings about your clients. Of course, beginning counselors may find it useful to enter counseling themselves. Supervision cannot be entirely concerned with the supervisee's issues, and personal counseling may facilitate the new counselor's growth as a therapist. You also gain the perspective of seeing what it's like to be on the other side of the counselor-client relationship.

3. Don't hide behind testing.

Because clients' expectations of counselors' expertise can influence the success of counseling (see Strong, 1968), beginning counselors may be tempted to boost their credibility through testing.

Counselor: (*authoritatively*) Your vocational test results indicate you should be a salesperson.

Client: Really?

Counselor: No doubt about it—look at these scores.

In this example, the counselor implies that the test is a foolproof method of selecting a career. Whereas testing data may be helpful in understanding clients and designing counseling strategies, the counselor should remember to explain the limits of the test along with the results (American Psychological Association, 1987). This caution is particularly important when tests are administered by computer; clients tend to view computer-administered instruments as more scientific (Herr & Best, 1984).

Counselor credibility comes with the confidence produced by experience and knowledge, not props. Being an expert does not mean that you are dogmatic or authoritarian (Cormier & Cormier, 1985).

Client: So which one of these careers on the computer list should I choose?

Counselor: Well, this inventory wasn't designed to make a choice for you. This list should help you get an idea of what kinds of careers might be best for you to explore.

Client: Oh.

Tests are tools. They are imperfect and useful at the same time. Test results, in and of themselves, never dictate action. Counselors employ tests as one more technique in their repertoire for helping clients.

4. On ethical questions, consult.

Counselors inevitably find themselves in gray zones. Counselors' duty to warn, confidentiality and privacy, client rights, and personal relationships with clients are issues with considerable potential for ambiguity and risk (Corey & Schneider Corey, 1987). In addition to knowing the formal ethical standards of your profession (see American Association for Counseling and Development, 1981; American Psychological

Association, 1987), you must be willing to discuss ethical issues with supervisors and colleagues.

Counselor 1:	He started to talk about wanting to hurt his ex-wife.
Counselor 2:	Did he mention a method?
Counselor 1:	I didn't think to ask about that. I'm wondering if I have to notify her about his threat.

States vary in the specifics of law, but in general, "duty to warn" refers to the legal responsibility of counselors to notify the persons that clients threaten (Schmidt & Meara, 1984). For example, if you were counseling a divorced man who threatened to kill his ex-wife, you would be legally obligated to contact and warn her about the threat. Obviously, such a warning breaks confidentiality, so counselors carefully assess the seriousness of threats made by clients. In general, you also have the obligation to protect clients' lives if they are suicidal and to report child abuse if you learn of it during counseling. Some agencies and counselors provide clients with a written form describing these limits to confidentiality, along with relevant information about clients' rights to terminate treatment and review records (Schmidt & Meara, 1984).

New counselors also express concern about the limits of their skill. Counselors refer clients they cannot help. New counselors may have difficulty deciding if they have the necessary skills. Consult with your supervisor when you begin to question whether you can help a particular client. Your supervisor may teach you new skills or help you find other assistance.

On ethical questions, don't get caught out on a limb. Always consult if you have any doubt. Colleagues and supervisors may be more objective and able to help you decide on an appropriate course of action.

CHAPTER 6

. . . .

A Brief
Introduction
to Intervention

Many counselors see therapy as primarily a relationship-building endeavor, but most emphasize the necessity of further intervention for change to occur (Egan, 1986). *How* to intervene effectively is an issue that divides today's counselors and psychotherapists.

Psychotherapists and counselors traditionally have discussed people in terms of three systems: affect, cognition, and behavior. "Affect" refers to the feelings we experience and express (such as anger or sadness); cognitions are the thoughts we think (for instance, "It's not my fault I flunked the test"); and behaviors are the overt acts we perform (such as smoking three packs of cigarettes a day). Clients frequently report that they seek counseling to change such painful feelings as anxiety or depression. However, systems of counseling and psychotherapy disagree vigorously about which of the three systems should be targeted for intervention. The task becomes further complicated by controversy about permanence of change (Mahoney, 1987) and the desynchrony of the systems (Rachman & Hodgson, 1974; Hodgson & Rachman, 1974). "Permanence of change" relates to the question of symptom substitution: if we change behavior without attention to underlying feelings or beliefs, will the problem resurface elsewhere? "Desynchrony" refers to the commonly observed lack of correspondence among measures of individuals' affect, cognitions, and behaviors. For example, even if clients change their behavior, weeks may pass before the corresponding change in feeling occurs.

Research findings support the general efficacy of counseling and psychotherapy (Smith & Glass, 1977; Landman & Dawes, 1982) but negate claims of overwhelming superiority for any one approach. Counselors still grapple with the question of which approach or counselor works best with which client or problem (Krumboltz, 1966). Rather than fighting battles over which approach is best, researchers have become increasingly interested in discerning common elements in different counseling approaches and theories (see Ivey, 1980, and Staats, 1983, for a fuller discussion).

Beginning counselors should become familiar with the basic theory and practice of many approaches. Only then can they make the informed choices necessary to create, integrate, and structure their personal method. The following list contains references for 11 well-known counseling approaches and provides a reasonable starting point for exploring the field.

1. Basic Counseling Texts

The following texts present overviews of various counseling approaches, counseling professions, and basic counseling skills. Elaboration of the content of *The Elements of Counseling* can be found in these books.

References

Corsini, R. (1984). *Current psychotherapies* (3rd ed.). Itasca, IL:: F.E. Peacock.

Egan, G. (1986). *The skilled helper: A systematic approach to effective helping* (3rd ed.). Pacific Grove, CA: Brooks/Cole.

Hansen, J., Stevic, R., & Warner, R. (1986). *Counseling: Theory and process*. Boston: Allyn & Bacon.

Ivey, A. (1988). *Intentional interviewing and counseling* (2nd ed.). Pacific Grove, CA: Brooks/Cole.

Osipow, S., Walsh, W. B., & Tosi, D. (1984). *A survey of counseling methods*. Homewood, IL: Dorsey Press.

Shertzer, B., & Stone, S. (1980). *Fundamentals of counseling* (3rd ed.). Boston: Houghton Mifflin.

Waldinger, R. (1986). *Fundamentals of psychiatry*. Washington, DC: American Psychiatric Press.

2. Person-Centered Counseling

Person-centered, client-centered, or nondirective therapy centers on the work of Carl Rogers. This approach is unique chiefly in its emphasis on clients' ability to determine relevant issues and to solve their problems. Person-centered counselors tend to see their clients positively (since all people are assumed to be striving for self-actualization) and to respond to clients with warmth, support, unconditional positive regard, genuineness, and empathy. Client-centered counselors assist clients in the change process by focusing predominantly on affect. The counselor notices client feelings and empathizes with those feelings to help clients fully experience their affects and become more open to their life experiences.

References
Meador, B. D., & Rogers, C. (1979). Person-centered therapy. In R. Corsini (Ed.), *Current psychotherapies* (2nd ed.). Itasca, IL: F. E. Peacock.

Patterson, C. H. (1985). *The therapeutic relationship: Foundations for an eclectic psychotherapy*. Pacific Grove, CA: Brooks/Cole.

Rogers, C. (1951). *Client-centered therapy*. Boston: Houghton Mifflin.

Rogers, C. (1986). Client-centered therapy. In I. Kutash & A. Wolk (Eds.), *Psychotherapist's casebook: Theory and technique in practice*. San Francisco: Jossey-Bass.

3. Behavioral Counseling

Behavioral counselors tend to be the pragmatists of the counseling profession. After all, they maintain, if it is behavior that we ultimately want to change (be it smoking, anxiety about school performance, or depression), then it is behavior we should target in counseling. Behavioral counselors focus on inappropriate learning as the source of client problems. Thus, clients may learn to inappropriately associate social situations with anxiety, and consequently a regimen of relaxation and assertiveness training is prescribed. Behavioral counselors pay attention to reinforcement as provided in clients' environments; if a child misbehaves at home, a behavioral counselor might teach parents about how to reward that child for more appropriate behavior.

References

Agras, W., Kazdin, A., & Wilson, G. (1979). *Behavior therapy.* San Francisco: W. H. Freeman.

Krumboltz, J., & Thoresen, C. (1976). *Counseling methods.* New York: Holt, Rinehart & Winston.

Masters, J., Burish, T., Hollon, S., & Rimm, D. (1987). *Behavior therapy: Techniques and empirical findings* (3rd ed.). San Diego, CA: Harcourt Brace Jovanovich.

Skinner, B. (1970). *Beyond freedom and dignity.* New York: Knopf.

Wilson, G., & Franks, C. (Eds.). (1982). *Contemporary behavior therapy.* New York: Guilford.

Wolpe, J. (1982). *The practice of behavior therapy* (3rd ed.). New York: Pergamon Press.

4. Cognitive and Cognitive-Behavioral Counseling

Cognitive and cognitive-behavioral counselors represent the latest movement in the counseling profession. In one form or another, these counselors see inappropriate thoughts as the cause of painful feelings and harmful behavior. Counselors like Ellis view irrational beliefs (beliefs without empirical evidence) as the target for interventions, while Beck describes how selective attention, magnifying problems, and illogical reasoning can lead to depression. Cognitive and cognitive-behavioral counseling grew from the behavioral counseling movement and share a tradition of respect for applying research to practice and doing counseling research.

References

Beck, A. (1976). *Cognitive therapies and the emotional disorders.* New York: International Universities Press.

Cormier, W., & Cormier, L. (1985). *Interviewing strategies for helpers: Fundamental skills and cognitive behavioral interventions* (2nd ed.). Pacific Grove, CA: Brooks/Cole.

Ellis, A., & Grieger, R. (1977). *Handbook of rational-emotive therapy.* New York: Springer.

Ellis, A., & Harper, R. (1976). *A new guide to rational living.* North Hollywood, CA: Wilshire Book Co.

Emery, G., Hollon, S., & Bedrosian, R. (Eds.). (1981). *New directions in cognitive therapy.* New York: Guilford.

Kelly, G. (1955). *The psychology of personal constructs.* New York: Norton.

Mahoney, M., & Arnkoff, D. (1978). Cognitive and self-control therapies. In S. Garfield & A. Bergin (Eds.), *Handbook of psychotherapy and behavior change: An empirical analysis.* New York: Wiley.

Meichenbaum, D. (1977). *Cognitive behavior modification: An integrative approach.* New York: Plenum.

Meichenbaum, D. (1985). *Stress-inoculation training.* New York: Pergamon Press.

Williamson, E. (1959). Some issues underlying counseling theory and practice. In W. Dugan (Ed.), *Counseling points of view.* Minneapolis: University of Minnesota Press.

5. Gestalt Counseling

Fritz Perls is the counselor most strongly associated with Gestalt counseling. Perls frustrated clients to help them move toward self-support and away from therapist support. Gestalt counselors also emphasize body movement as a method of experiencing feelings and facilitating psychological growth. Like person-centered counselors, Gestalt counselors pay particular attention to noticing client feelings, staying in the here-and-now, and avoiding intellectual analysis of problems.

References

Downing, J. (1976). *Gestalt awareness.* New York: Harper & Row.

Perls, F. (1970). *In and out of the garbage can.* New York: Bantam.

Perls, F. (1971). *Gestalt therapy verbatim.* New York: Bantam Books.

Perls, F., Hefferline, R., & Goodman, P. (1977). *Gestalt therapy: Excitement and growth in the human personality.* New York: Bantam.

Polster, E., & Polster, M. (1973). *Gestalt therapy integrated.* New York: Brunner/Mazel.

Zinker, J. (1977). *Creative process in Gestalt therapy.* New York: Random House.

6. Transactional Analysis

One of the strengths of transactional analysis (TA) is its relatively simple view of personality and interpersonal interaction. TA counselors suggest that each individual is composed of three parts: Parent, Adult, and Child. Our Parent tells us what is right; our Adult makes decisions and tests reality; and our Child plays and has needs. Part of TA counseling involves teaching this personality theory, which is easy for clients to learn and remember. Conflict among Parent, Adult, and Child explains both intrapsychic and interpersonal difficulties. For example, adults often find that their parents still view them as children and are incapable of communicating adult-to-adult with them. TA counselors help their clients achieve a balance among their three parts, with a slight emphasis on the decision-making Adult. A person with too much Child would likely have difficulty living a responsible life; a person with too much Parent might have difficulty enjoying life.

References

Berne, E. (1978). *Transactional analysis in psychotherapy.* New York: Ballantine.

Goulding, R., & Goulding, M. (1978). *The power is in the patient.* San Francisco: TA Press.

Harris, T. (1982). *I'm OK—You're OK.* New York: Avon.

Jongeward, D., & Scott, D. (1976). *Women as winners: Transactional analysis for personal growth.* Reading, MA: Addison-Wesley.

Steiner, C. (1974). *Scripts people live: Transactional analysis of life scripts.* New York: Grove Press.

Woollams, S., & Brown, M. (1978). *Transactional analysis.* Dexter, MI: Huron Valley Institute Press.

7. Psychoanalytic Counseling

Sigmund Freud set the foundation from which all counseling approaches evolved. His ideas about the unconscious and personality development led to ingenious counseling techniques, and motivated opponents to create such radically different approaches as behavioral counseling and rational-emotive therapy. Much of the work of the psychoanalytic counselor involves making unconscious material conscious, thereby helping counselor and client to gain insight into the mechanisms of psychological adjustment. However, this process is frequently anxiety provoking to clients who resist self-awareness by means of various defense mechanisms. More than exponents of any other approach, psychoanalytic counselors emphasize the role of past parent-child transactions and foster the recreation of this relationship in counseling. Clients' feelings toward their parents, projected onto the counselor, are called *transference.* By bringing transference into the open, clients gain new understanding of their psychological processes and ameliorate troubling symptoms.

References
Brill, A. (Ed.). (1938). *The basic writings of Sigmund Freud.* New York: Modern Library.

Freud, A. (1946). *The ego and the mechanisms of defense.* New York: International Universities Press.

Jung, C. (1959). *Basic writings.* New York: Modern Library.

Kernberg, O. (1981). *Object relations theory and clinical psychoanalysis.* New York: Aronson.

Langs, R. (1973). *The techniques of psychoanalytic psychotherapy* (Vol. 1). New York: Aronson.

Malcolm, J. (1981). *Psychoanalysis, the impossible profession.* New York: Knopf.

Menninger, K. (1958). *Theory of psychoanalytic technique.* New York: Basic Books.

Shapiro, D. (1965). *Neurotic styles.* New York: Basic Books.

St. Clair, M. (1987). *Object relations and self psychology: An introduction.* Pacific Grove, CA: Brooks/Cole.

Strupp, H., & Binder, J. (1985). *Psychotherapy in a new key: A guide to time-limited dynamic psychotherapy.* New York: Basic Books.

Wachtel, P. (1977). *Psychoanalysis and behavior therapy: Toward an integration.* New York: Basic Books.

8. Existential Counseling

Existential counselors examine the role of what many consider abstract philosophical issues in the psychological lives of individuals. More than adherents of any other approach, existential counselors eschew technique in favor of grappling with the basic dimensions of life and death.

Thus, people can be considered in terms of being (which corresponds to an awareness of oneself) and nonbeing (a loss of identity, perhaps caused by conformity). Rollo May, an eminent existential counselor, describes anxiety as the experience of the threat of imminent nonbeing. Like person-centered and Gestalt counselors, existentialists see personal choice and volition as basic facts of human existence. To existential counselors, clients seek counseling to expand their psychological worlds. The job of the existential counselor is to be authentic, to expose oneself to clients so that they can become aware of similar qualities in themselves. Like many behaviorists, existential counselors believe that knowledge and insight *follow* behavior change, not vice versa.

References

Frankl, V. (1985). *Man's search for meaning*. New York: Washington Square Press.

Jourard, S. (1971). *The transparent self* (rev. ed.). New York: Van Nostrand Reinhold.

Keen, E. (1970). *Three faces of being: Toward an existential clinical psychology*. New York: Appleton-Century-Crofts.

May, R. (1983). *The discovery of being*. New York: Norton.

Sartre, J.P. (1971). *Being and nothingness*. New York: Bantam.

Watson, R. (1977). An introduction to humanistic psychotherapy. In S. Morse & R. Watson (Eds.), *Psychotherapies: A comparative casebook*. New York: Holt, Rinehart & Winston.

9. Social Learning

Social learning counselors closely resemble cognitive and cognitive-behavioral counselors. Both groups emphasize the importance of cognitions in human behavior. Social learning counselors, however, tend to focus specifically on individuals' expectations. As a result of their social experiences, individuals learn to expect that (a) some events are more personally rewarding that others; (b) certain behaviors can produce desired events, although there may be events that are uncontrollable; and (c) people differ in their feelings of competence for doing the behaviors that can produce desired events. Although expectations are viewed as the driving force, social-learning theorists often do not directly intercede with cognitions. Instead, they modify clients' expectations through actual performance (such as by gradual exposure to increasingly fearful situations, as is done with snake phobics) or through use of models who demonstrate skilled behavior.

References

Bandura, A. (1969). *Principles of behavior modification*. New York: Holt, Rinehart & Winston.

Bandura, A. (1977a). Self-efficacy theory: Toward a unifying view of behavioral change. *Psychological Review, 84,* 191-215.

Bandura, A. (1977b). *Social learning theory.* Englewood Cliffs, NJ: Prentice-Hall.

Mischel, W. (1986). *Introduction to personality* (4th ed.). New York: Holt, Rinehart & Winston.

Rosenthal, T., & Zimmerman, B. (1978). *Social learning and cognition.* New York: Academic Press.

Rotter, J. (1954). *Social learning and clinical psychology.* Englewood Cliffs, NJ: Prentice-Hall.

Rotter, J. (1971). *Clinical psychology* (2nd ed.). Englewood Cliffs, NJ: Prentice-Hall.

Rotter, J., Chance, J., & Phares, E. (1972). *Applications of a social learning theory of personality.* New York: Holt, Rinehart & Winston.

10. Group Counseling

Group counselors may subscribe to any of the counseling approaches described above; that is, you may find Gestalt groups, person-centered groups, and cognitive-behavioral groups. What all group counselors share in common is a recognition of the benefits of working with more than one client at a time.

If clients can be placed in a group on the basis of relatively similar problems, this modality is efficient in comparison with one-to-one counseling. In most groups, benefits occur from interactions among group members, not from working with the counselor per se. With therapeutic groups, the group counselor is more a facilitator than an active participant or leader. Skilled group counselors supply moderate amounts of group rules and emotional challenges along with high amounts of support and interpretation of group processes (Lieberman, Yalom, & Miles, 1973).

References

Gazda, G. (1984). *Group counseling: A developmental approach* (3rd ed.). Boston: Allyn & Bacon.

Hansen, J., Warner, R., & Smith, E. (1980). *Group counseling: Theory and process* (2nd ed.). Boston: Houghton Mifflin.

Schneider Corey, M., & Corey, G. (1987). *Groups: Process and practice (3rd ed.).* Pacific Grove, CA: Brooks/Cole.

Yalom, I. (1985). *The theory and practice of group psychotherapy* (3rd ed.). New York: Basic Books.

11. Family/Systems Counseling

Family and systems approaches represent a relatively new approach to counseling. In contrast to traditional methods, which focus on processes within the individual as the target of change, family and systems counselors chart the influence of social systems on clients. The goal of the family counselor is to detect and understand the methods family members use to communicate among themselves, maintain the family structure, and help or hinder members' growth. Many systems counselors share with Gestalt counselors an interest in psycholinguistics, the study of how language influences what we think, do, and feel.

References

Bandler, R., & Grinder, J. (1975). *The structure of magic.* Palo Alto, CA: Science and Behavior Books.

Bateson, G. (1972). *Steps to an ecology of mind.* New York: Ballantine.

Bowen, M. (1978). *Family therapy in clinical practice.* New York: Aronson.

deShazer, S. (1982). *Patterns of brief family therapy.* New York: Guilford.

Haley, J. (1987). *Problem-solving therapy* (2nd ed.). San Francisco: Jossey-Bass.

Madanes, C. (1984). *Behind the one-way mirror: Advances in the practice of strategic therapy.* San Francisco: Jossey-Bass.

Minuchin, S., & Fishman, H. C. (1981). *Family therapy techniques.* Cambridge, MA: Harvard University Press.

Napier, A., & Whitaker, C. (1978). *The family crucible.* New York: Harper & Row.

Satir, V., & Baldwin, M. (1983). *Satir step by step.* Palo Alto, CA: Science and Behavior Books.

Watzlawick, P., Weakland, J., & Fisch, R. (1974). *Change: Principles of problem formation and problem resolution.* New York: Norton.

12. Research on Counseling and Psychotherapy

Research in counseling focuses on process and outcome. The basic outcome question is this: Is counseling effective? Most would say yes on the basis of previous research. Perhaps the best result of all the research conducted in counseling and psychotherapy is that we are continually asking better questions (for example, what client characteristics interact with what type of treatment to produce the best outcome?) and we are continually improving the sophistication of the research employed to seek answers to these questions.

Unfortunately, one might argue that improved research sophistication is the most detectable outcome of past decades of counseling research. That is, relatively few counselors pay attention to research past their training years, partially because research results often appear to add little to current practice. However, research, theory, and practice must be increasingly integrated if counseling is to progress as a science.

References
Cummings, N., & Follette, W. (1968). Psychiatric services and medical utilization in a pre-paid health plan setting. *Medical Care, 5,* 31-41.

Eysenck, H. (1952). The effects of psychotherapy: An evaluation. *Journal of Consulting Psychology, 16,* 319-324.

Garfield, S., & Bergin, A. (1986). *Handbook of psychotherapy and behavior change: An empirical analysis* (3rd ed). New York: Wiley.

Gelso, C. (1979). Research in counseling: Methodological and professional issues. *The Counseling Psychologist, 8,* 7-35.

Glass, G., & Kliegl, R. (1984). An apology for research integration in the study of psychotherapy. *Journal of Consulting and Clinical Psychology, 51,* 28-41.

Rachman, S., & Wilson, G. (1980). *The effects of psychological therapy.* New York: Wiley.

Smith, M., & Glass, G. (1977). Meta-analysis of psychotherapy outcome studies. *American Psychologist, 32,* 752-760.

13. Other Important Sources

Not all important publications fit neatly into the categories already listed. The following sources are also worthy of your attention.

References
Adler, A. (1969). *The practice and theory of individual psychology* (2nd ed.). Totowa, NJ: Littlefield.

American Psychiatric Association. (1987). *Diagnostic and statistical manual of mental disorders* (3rd ed., rev.). Washington, DC: Author.

Glasser, W. (1975). *Reality therapy.* New York: Harper & Row.

Lazarus, A. (1981). *The practice of multi-modal therapy.* New York: McGraw-Hill.

Zeig, J. (1987). *The evolution of psychotherapy.* New York: Brunner/Mazel.

References

Abramowitz, S., Weitz, L., Schwartz, J., Amura, S., Gomes, B., & Abramowitz, C. (1975). Comparative counselor inferences toward women with medical school aspirations. *Journal of College Student Personnel, 16,* 128-130.

American Association for Counseling and Development. (1981). *Ethical standards.* Alexandria, VA: Author.

American Psychological Association. (1987). Ethical principles of psychologists. In *Directory of the American Psychological Association.* Washington, DC: Author.

Anton, J., Dunbar, J., & Friedman, L. (1976). Anticipation training in the treatment of depression. In J. Krumboltz & C. Thoresen (Eds.), *Counseling methods.* New York: Holt, Rinehart & Winston.

Applied Innovations (1985). *Client progress notes* [Computer program]. Wakefield, RI: Author.

Bandler, R., & Grinder, J. (1975). *The structure of magic.* Palo Alto, CA: Science and Behavior Books.

Bandura, A. (1977). Self-efficacy theory: Toward a unifying view of behavioral change. *Psychological Review, 84,* 191-215.

Barrett-Lennard, G. (1974). Experiential learning groups. *Psychotherapy: Theory, Research and Practice, 11,* 71-75.

Bartlett, W., Goodyear, R., & Bradley, F. (Eds.). (1983). Supervision in counseling II. *The Counseling Psychologist, 11*(1).

Bednar, R., & Kaul, T. (1978). Experiential group research: Current perspectives. In S. Garfield & A. Bergin (Eds.), *Handbook of psychotherapy and behavior change: An empirical analysis.* New York: Wiley.

Bergin, A., & Lambert, M. (1978). The evaluation of therapeutic outcomes. In S. Garfield & A. Bergin (Eds.), *Handbook of psychotherapy and behavior change: An empirical analysis.* New York: Wiley.

Betz, N., & Hackett, G. (1981). The relationships of career-related self-efficacy expectations to perceived career options in college women and men. *Journal of Counseling Psychology, 28,* 399-410.

Butcher, J., & Koss, M. (1978). Research on brief and crisis-oriented psychotherapies. In S. Garfield & A. Bergin (Eds.), *Handbook of psychotherapy and behavior change: An empirical analysis.* New York: Wiley.

Brammer, L., & Shostrom, E. (1982). *Therapeutic psychology* (4th ed.). Englewood Cliffs, NJ: Prentice-Hall.

Caplan, G. (1961). *An approach to community mental health.* New York: Grune & Stratton.

Casas, J. M. (1984). Policy, training, and research in counseling psychology: The racial/ethnic minority perspective. In S. Brown & R. Lent (Eds.), *Handbook of counseling psychology.* New York: Wiley.

Corey, G., & Schneider Corey, M. (1987). *Issues and ethics in the helping professions* (2nd ed.). Pacific Grove, CA: Brooks/Cole.

Cormican, J. (1978, March). Linguistic issues in interviewing. *Social Casework,* 145-151.

Cormier, W., & Cormier, L. (1985). *Interviewing strategies for helpers: Fundamental skills and cognitive behavioral interventions* (2nd ed.). Pacific Grove, CA: Brooks/Cole.

Davis, S. (1987, December 14). Personal communication.

deShazer, S. (1982). *Patterns of brief family therapy.* New York: Guilford.

Durlak, J. (1979). Comparative effectiveness of paraprofessional and professional helpers. *Psychological Bulletin, 86,* 80-92.

Dweck, C. (1986). Motivational processes affecting learning. *American Psychologist, 41,* 1040-1048.

Egan, G. (1986). *The skilled helper: A systematic approach to effective helping* (3rd ed.). Pacific Grove, CA: Brooks/Cole.

Eisler, R. (1976). Assertive training in the work situation. In J. Krumboltz & C. Thoresen (Eds.), *Counseling methods.* New York: Holt, Rinehart & Winston.

Ellis, A., & Grieger, R. (1977). *Handbook of rational-emotive therapy.* New York: Springer.

Ellis, A., & Harper, R. (1976). *A new guide to rational living.* North Hollywood, CA: Wilshire Book Co.

Forsyth, D., & Strong, S. (1986). The scientific study of counseling and psychotherapy: A unificationist view. *American Psychologist, 41,* 113-119.

Frank, J. (1971). Therapeutic factors in psychotherapy. *American Journal of Psychotherapy, 25,* 350-361.

Freudenberger, H. (1974). Staff burnout. *Journal of Social Issues, 30,* 159-165.

Gelso, C. (1979). Research in counseling: Methodological and professional issues. *The Counseling Psychologist, 8,* 7-35.

Gilbert, L. A., & Waldroop, J. (1978). Evaluation of a procedure for increasing sex-fair counseling. *Journal of Counseling Psychology, 25,* 410-418.

Goldfried, M. R. (1983). The behavior therapist in clinical practice. *Behavior Therapist, 6,* 45-46.

Goldman, L. (1976). A revolution in counseling research. *Journal of Counseling Psychology, 23,* 543-552.

Gordon, D. (1978). *Therapeutic metaphors.* Cupertino, CA: Meta Publications.

Greenson, R. (1965). The working alliance and the transference neurosis. *Psychoanalytic Quarterly, 34,* 155-181.

Gunzburger, D., Henggeler, S., & Watson, S. (1985). Factors related to premature termination of counseling relationships. *Journal of College Student Personnel, 26,* 456-460.

Gurman, A., & Kniskern, D. (1978). Research on marital and family therapy: Progress, perspective, and prospect. In S. Garfield & A. Bergin (Eds.), *Handbook of psychotherapy and behavior change: An empirical analysis.* New York: Wiley.

Hansen, J., Stevic, R., & Warner, R. (1986). *Counseling: Theory and process.* Boston: Allyn & Bacon.

Helms, J. (1979). Perceptions of a sex-fair counselor and her client. *Journal of Counseling Psychology, 26,* 504-513.

Herr, E., & Best, P. (1984). Computer technology and counseling: The role of the profession. *Journal of Counseling and Development, 63,* 192-195.

Hodgson, R., & Rachman, S. (1974). II. Desynchrony in measures of fear. *Behaviour Research and Therapy, 12,* 319-326.

Hoehn-Saric, R., Frank, J., Imber, S., Nash, E., Stone, A., & Battle, C. (1964). Systematic preparation of patients for psychotherapy: I. Effects on therapy behavior and outcome. *Journal of Psychiatric Research, 2,* 267-281.

Instructional Enterprises. (1984). *Counselor log* [Computer program]. Minneapolis: Educational Media Corporation.

Ivey, A. (1980). Counseling 2000: Time to take charge! *The Counseling Psychologist, 8,* 12-16.

Jourard, S. (1971). *Self-disclosure: An experimental analysis of the transparent self.* New York: Wiley.

Karasu, T. (1986). The specificity versus nonspecificity dilemma: Toward identifying therapeutic change agents. *American Journal of Psychiatry, 143,* 698-695.

Kiesler, D. J. (1971). Experimental designs in psychotherapy research. In A. Bergin & S. Garfield (Eds.), *Handbook of psychotherapy and behavior change.* New York: Wiley.

Kilburg, R., Nathan, P., & Thoreson, R. (1986). *Professionals in distress.* Washington, DC: American Psychological Association.

Krumboltz, J. (Ed.). (1966). *Revolution in counseling.* Boston: Houghton Mifflin.

Kuhn, T. (1962). *The structure of scientific revolutions.* Chicago: University of Chicago Press.

Landman, J., & Dawes, R. (1982). Psychotherapy outcome. *American Psychologist, 37,* 504-516.

Langs, R. (1973). *The techniques of psychoanalytic psychotherapy* (Vol. 1). New York: Aronson.

Lieberman, M., Yalom, I., & Miles, M. (1973). *Encounter groups: First facts.* New York: Basic Books.

MacKinnon, R., & Michels, R. (1971). *The psychiatric interview in clinical practice.* Philadelphia: Saunders.

Mahoney, M. (1987, August). *Plasticity and power: Emerging emphases in theories of human change.* Paper presented at the 95th Annual Meeting of the American Psychological Assoc., New York.

Mayerson, N. (1984). Preparing clients for group therapy: A critical review and theoretical formulation. *Clinical Psychology Review, 4,* 191-213.

McCarthy, P. (1982). Differential effects of counselor self-referent responses and counselor status. *Journal of Counseling Psychology, 29,* 125-131.

McCarthy, P., & Betz, N. (1978). Differential effects of self-disclosing versus self-involving counselor statements. *Journal of Counseling Psychology, 25,* 251-256.

Meehl, P. (1956). Wanted—A good cookbook. *American Psychologist, 11,* 262-272.

Meehl, P. (1973). Why I no longer attend clinical case conferences. In *Psychodiagnosis: Selected papers.* Minneapolis: University of Minnesota Press.

Meier, S. (1983). Toward a theory of burnout. *Human Relations, 36,* 899-910.

Meier, S. (1987). An unconnected special issue. *American Psychologist, 42,* 881.

Minuchin, S. (1974). *Families and family therapy.* Cambridge, MA: Harvard University Press.

Orlinsky, D., & Howard, K. (1978). The relation of process to outcome in psychotherapy. In S. Garfield & A. Bergin (Eds.), *Handbook of psychotherapy and behavior change: An empirical analysis.* New York: Wiley.

Pope, B. (1979). *The mental health interview.* New York: Pergamon Press.

Puryear, D. (1979). *Helping people in crisis.* San Francisco: Jossey-Bass.

Rachman, S., & Hodgson, R. (1974). Synchrony and desynchrony in fear and avoidance. *Behaviour Research and Therapy, 12,* 311-318.

Richardson, M., & Johnson, M. (1984). Counseling women. In S. Brown & R. Lent (Eds.), *Handbook of counseling psychology.* New York: Wiley.

Robertiello, R., & Schoenewolf, G. (1987). *101 Common therapeutic blunders.* Northvale, NJ: Aronson.

Rogers, C. (1963). Psychotherapy today, or where do we go from here? *American Journal of Psychotherapy, 17,* 5-16.

Rosenthal, D., & Frank, J. (1958). Psychotherapy and the placebo effect. In C. Reed, I. Alexander, & S. Tomkins (Eds.), *Psychopathology: A source book.* Cambridge, MA: Harvard University Press.

Russell, R. (1970). Black perceptions of guidance. *Personnel & Guidance Journal, 48,* 721-728.

Satir, V. (1972). *People-making.* Palo Alto, CA: Science and Behavior Books.

Schmidt, L., & Meara, N. (1984). Ethical, professional, and legal issues in counseling psychology. In S. Brown & R. Lent (Eds.), *Handbook of counseling psychology.* New York: Wiley.

Schneider Corey, M., & Corey, G. (1987). *Groups: Process and practice* (3rd ed.). Pacific Grove, CA: Brooks/Cole.

Shertzer, B., & Stone, S. (1980). *Fundamentals of counseling* (3rd ed.). Boston: Houghton Mifflin.

Slaikeu, K. (1984). *Crisis intervention.* Boston: Allyn & Bacon.

Smith, M., & Glass, G. (1977). Meta-analysis of psychotherapy outcome studies. *American Psychologist, 32,* 752-760.

Staats, A. (1983). *Psychology's crisis of disunity: Philosophy and method for a unified science.* New York: Praeger.

Strong, S. (1968). Counseling: An interpersonal influence process. *Journal of Counseling Psychology, 15,* 215-224.

Strunk, W., Jr., & White, E. B. (1979). *The elements of style* (3rd ed.). New York: Macmillan.

Stuart, R. (1974). Teaching facts about drugs: Pushing or preventing? *Journal of Educational Psychology, 66,* 189-201.

Sue, D. W. (1978). Eliminating cultural oppression in counseling: Toward a general theory. *Journal of Counseling Psychology, 25,* 419-428.

Sullivan, H. S. (1970). *The psychiatric interview.* New York: Norton.

Van Kaam, A. (1966). *The art of existential counseling.* Wilkes-Barre, PA: Dimension Books.

Varenhorst, B. (1984). Peer counseling: Past promises, current status, and future directions. In S. Brown & R. Lent (Eds.), *Handbook of counseling psychology.* New York: Wiley.

Watzlawick, P., Weakland, J., & Fisch, R. (1974). *Change: Principles of problem formation and problem resolution.* New York: Norton.

Whiteley, J. (Ed.). (1982). Supervision in counseling I. *The Counseling Psychologist, 10*(1).

Wolpe, J. (1982). *The practice of behavior therapy* (3rd ed.). New York: Pergamon Press.

Yalom, I. (1985). *The theory and practice of group psychotherapy* (3rd ed.). New York: Basic Books.

Zetzel, E. (1956). Current concepts of transference. *International Journal of Psychoanalysis, 37*, 369-376.

Index